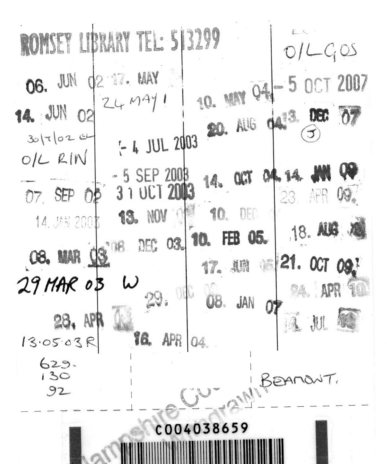

The Years Flew Past

40 Years at the Leading Edge of Aviation

TheYears Flew Past

40 Years at the Leading Edge of Aviation

XG3IO

ROLAND 'BEE' BEAMONT

Airlife

England

First published in the UK in 2001
by Airlife Publishing Ltd

British Library Cataloguing-in-Publication Data
A catalogue record for this book
is available from the British Library

ISBN 1 84037 299 0

Typeset by Rowland Phototypesetting Ltd,
Bury St Edmunds, Suffolk
Printed in England by MPG Books Ltd., Bodmin, Cornwall

Airlife Publishing Ltd
101 Longden Road, Shrewsbury, SY3 9EB, England
E-mail: airlife@airlifebooks.com
Website: www.airlifebooks.com

Other books by the same author:

Phoenix into Ashes William Kimber
Typhoon and Tempest at War (with Arthur Reed) Ian Allan
Testing Years Ian Allan
English Electric Canberra (with Arthur Reed) Ian Allan
English Electric P1 Lightning Ian Allan
Fighter Test Pilot PSL
My Part of the Sky PSL
Testing Early Jets Airlife
Tempest over Europe Airlife
Flying to the Limit PSL

For Pat

For fifty-four years of my life, best-ever friend and companion and wonderful mother of our family.

She wanted so much that this book should be written, but sadly it will be the poorer for lack of her always incisive, shrewd and laughing interventions, and her fond and admiring memories of people.

DEDICATION

To all those who strove in war and peace to produce some of the world's finest aircraft for our armed forces; to the pilots and crews who made such formidable use of them in the Services, and to the splendid Warton test pilots, navigators and observers who flew with me in Britain's first supersonic test team.

ACKNOWLEDGEMENTS

Grateful thanks are due to the sources listed under Bibliography; to Joan Moores for her patient diligence in interpreting and typing my often indecipherable manuscripts; and especially to my daughter Billy Richardson for her shrewd, disciplinary but always helpful criticism and supportive advice.

CONTENTS

PROLOGUE

Octber 1944.

The small figure in front of the Control tower waved as I taxied my Tempest 'RB' towards Dunsfold's main runway.

Shirley had been unwell during our so-brief weekend together with baby Carol, and I had asked her to be sure to see a doctor. We had been married only two years, but now I had to fly out to rejoin my Wing at Volkel in Holland for the battles for Germany. I had assured Shirley that I would soon be home as my third 'tour of operations' had already lasted seven months and a 'rest period', which I had certainly not wanted until then, could not be far away.

Three days later my Tempest was hit by groundfire over Germany and I became a prisoner of war, cut off in every way from any chance of caring for Shirley and the baby – an agony to live with every day and night for the next seven months until finally released by the Russians from our Potsdam POW camp.

I landed at RAF Oakley near Oxford, in June 1945 in a Bomber Command Lancaster crammed with returning POWs, and going straight to the Officers' Mess telephoned my home near Chichester where I hoped my parents and my wife and baby Carol would be.

My father's choked voice said, 'My God, how am I to tell him?' and then, 'Shirley died in hospital two weeks ago.' Shirley, so beautiful, young and vibrant, so proud of the RAF and of me and of our baby Carol. So loving of life. We had managed to be together for only six months of our two-year marriage, and then I had not seen or heard from her for those seven long months in prison camps.

Now she did not exist. It was just unbelievable.

In the void that followed I must have been granted leave at Chichester to ensure that baby Carol was safe in the fond care of her mother's parents, and one day my dear Mother said, 'You must get out and see people', and she dispatched me to a party of old friends and acquaintances whom I had not seen since the pre-war 1930s.

It was a pleasant gathering and on the tennis court some young people were knocking balls about amid peals of laughter. Among them was a lovely girl, bronzed and golden-haired in tennis whites, who seemed to be having a splendid time. I watched her for a while and then she came over to our group for a cold drink.

Someone introduced us (as was customary in those days) and suddenly she got up, waved a racket at me and said, 'Come on, let's have a game!'

I protested slightly saying that I did not really play tennis, and she said, 'Oh yes you do!' and in the next minutes cannon balls were whistling round my ears from all directions!

Not willing to be easily defeated I launched a counter-attack with volleys into the net, high in the air, over the surrounding court netting, and pretty well everywhere except in my opponent's court. Eventually with more peals of laughter we sought cool drinks and deck-chairs.

I saw her the next day, and the day after that, and I was soon counting the hours every day until our next meeting.

We swam at Wittering and walked the Sussex downs at Goodwood that summer. We watched the evening skies over the Isle of Wight and along to Selsey Bill where I could still imagine seeing the great skeins of Spitfires spiralling for height over Sussex as the Tangmere Wing set course for the Battle for Normandy over a year before. And always we talked and talked until one day my leave was ending.

Pat had had a terrible war, striving to save her son Richard's failing sight by taking jobs in London throughout the bombing of the Blitz and later the fierce Flying Bombs attack in 1944 in order to be able to take the boy to and from Moorfields Eye Hospital whenever necessary.

Our situation was complex but now we were facing separation. One late evening on the Downs I said, 'When we can sort all this out, will you marry me?' 'Of course,' she said quietly as if the question had not been necessary but that it was nice to be asked.

And so we talked and laughed and talked for over fifty-four years. It was from the beginning as if we had always known each other and that our meeting had been ordained. I told her that I would always take care of her, but after all those wonderful years I was not able to any longer when, surrounded by her loving daughters, she died in my arms.

Pat who shared all our fortunes and misfortunes with such strength and laughter; who created our wonderful family with so much love and wisdom; and supported all my puny endeavours with such determination and courage, and who lived a life of dedicated duty, loyalty and caring which so surely guided us all. Pat was the determined inspiration and taskmaster for this book.

Had she lived, this would have contained infinitely more laughs from her limitless recollections of the hilarity and warmth in human nature.

INTRODUCTION

1 939–1999. The years flew past. A momentous period in world history and in the history of aviation, and I was so fortunate to be involved in a very small way in many stirring events in this period.

Serving in RAF Fighter Command in the Battles of France and Britain in 1940, and in the campaigns across the Channel in 1941, '42, '43 and the ultimate battles in 1944 for Normandy and Germany.

Experimental testing the formidable Typhoon and Tempest fighters and then taking them into action.

Testing the evocative new jet-era fighters and bombers post-war, and then the first British truly supersonic fighters and flying them for the first time to supersonic speeds in level flight and ultimately to twice the speed of sound (the Lightning).

Then testing the technically brilliant but politically ill-fated TSR2 strike aircraft for the RAF, and flying it ultimately to supersonic speed.

Responsibility for Lightning operations in the desert for many years in the great British programme for the supersonic defence of Saudi Arabia, 'Al Yamamah'.

Board level involvements in the international programmes for the Jaguar and Tornado fighter-bombers; and before all these, wide-ranging flying displays and sales tours at home and abroad with the immensely successful English Electric jet bomber which made its powerfully effective public debut at the Farnborough Air Display of 1949 and is still in RAF service in 1999 – the first aircraft type to serve in the RAF for fifty years and with more to come!

Through all those years and events there was one central and outstanding feature – the quality, dedication and sheer good-humoured 'go for it' attitudes of my peers and colleagues.

The fighter pilots of 1940–45 were a joy to be with, and the scale of their achievements was often humbling in comparison with one's own puny and inexperienced efforts. This was particularly so during the Battle of Britain.

Our leaders and colleagues were always a source of inspiration which remains to this day.

By 1944 the great fighter leaders, most by then personal friends, had achieved so much with calm, capable and at times uproariously humorous confidence in their abilities to lead their squadrons and wings in the Invasion of Europe, as to raise within me doubts as to whether I would be able to cope in that way when, at age twenty-three, leading my own Tempest Wing into battle in 1944.

But I had their example and that of most of my own splendid earlier commanders to follow. The inspiration was always there and I have carried the memory of their friendship and exceptional standards of duty and honour with me to this day.

And then the jets and the supersonic era. The arrival of practical jet propulsion in the 1940s brought with it a step-change in aircraft design and the imminent possibility of advancing performance to the speed of sound and beyond.

It had been my good fortune to be in at the beginning, taking part in the earliest research flying into the problems of loss of control in 'compressibility' as the speed of sound was approached, and then first-flying the first British supersonic fighters and bombers and finally taking them for the first time to Mach 1 and Mach 2.

In all of this, in war and peace, the sheer quality of the people at the cutting edge (though sadly not always at levels in the Establishment) was a constant inspiration.

In war the ground crews working tirelessly and with little recognition in all weathers and often under enemy fire; the aircrews facing immense danger every day and night, apparently as a matter of course; and the warmly humorous yet aggressive leaders up through all the chains of command to the great chiefs at Group and Command levels, were an indomitable combination. Morale in the RAF was formidable, and the team spirit inspiring and unbeatable as our enemies found to their cost.

With the peace, the great challenge of the supersonic era brought out similar qualities of dedication, patriotism, loyalty and sheer determination to achieve not just the best for Britain but the best aircraft in the world, and these qualities immediately became apparent in the factories and design offices of the builders.

The new jets were dramatic and successful, and in the 1950s British aviation became the world leader with even the great USAF buying our Canberras (licence-built in America) because they themselves could make nothing as good at that period; and Canberras equipped fifteen other air forces worldwide.

In my company, English Electric, there seemed to be no end in the decades of the '50s and '60s to the successes of the Canberra, P1 and Lightning until, when developing the BAC TSR2 supersonic bomber for the RAF, we came up against a sudden and impenetrable wall. The TSR2 was, soon after successfully exceeding Mach 1, cancelled peremptorily and without Parliamentary debate at the very point of technical success by politicians who clearly did not understand what they were meddling with.

Following the cancellation, in the consequent national uproar the politicians denied all responsibility. But the ministers involved and their departments were collectively responsible for eliminating completely for the next twenty years the crucial long-range strike and reconnaissance effectiveness of the RAF.

They were culpable of depleting the national defence capability over a significant period. They should have been indicted for this and heads should have rolled.

It was not until the 1980s that the RAF recovered part of this capability with the introduction into NATO of the successful international Panavia Tornado, but in some respects the Tornado's performance still fell significantly short of that of the cancelled TSR2 of twenty years before!

But with only a few exceptions it had all been a powerful and positive experience. From the Hurricanes and Spitfires in the Battle of Britain to the Tornadoes of the NATO forces in the 1990s we had supplied fine high-quality aircraft to the RAF, and many of the types had no superiors anywhere in the world.

The Royal Air Force enjoyed our aircraft and we had enjoyed providing them.

Occasionally accolades were bestowed for these achievements, but in the main the feeling of a job well done was reward enough for the many thousands involved in the industry. But there was one shortfall in recognition from any level. The unsung, dedicated support given always as a matter of course by the wives to husbands working long, late hours; the disrupted weekends and late-cancelled holidays, and long separations when husbands travelled the world on support missions; and in particular the wives of test pilots and test aircrew who were always the first to say that their lot was no different from the others, when in fact they knew full well that they only would each be facing almost daily silent fears that one day their man would not be coming home from one of the inevitable 'high risk' category test flights. The house would then have only herself and the children, and what of the future?

There were seldom accolades for this.

In the following pages just a few of the events of these exciting times are recalled, some serious, some distinctly less so and some indeed hilarious. They all added up to a wonderful experience for which I shall always be profoundly grateful.

CHAPTER ONE

WORLD WAR II

The Fighters in the Battle of Britain

The air battle which changed the course of history

From 10 May 1940, the Hurricane squadrons of the Air component of the British Expeditionary Force in France became locked in combat with the powerful and war-experienced air arm of the German invasion force, the Luftwaffe.

The fighting was intense in the air as the enemy Panzer army advanced their *Blitzkrieg* across northern France, reaching the Somme estuary beyond Abbeville on 20 May and splitting the French army in the west from the British and Belgian forces in the north-east. The battle for France was lost.

Many hundreds of Hurricanes were shot down or destroyed by bombing on our French airfields and a myth began to emerge about the invincibility of the Messerschmitt 109. This did not arise from the fighter pilots themselves who regarded their losses as being due to the enemy's superiority in numbers. The 109s were thought to be merely competent fighters, although flown by mainly combat-experienced pilots which none of us were. That gave them a possible edge but not to a menacing extent.

No. 87 Squadron's first victory in France, November 1939 near Lille. Dennis David on the wing.

The pilots and ground crew at Lille Séclin. Author (RPB on jacket) centre-right.

Nevertheless, with the forced withdrawal of our forces from France at the end of May when it became immediately clear that there would be only a month or at the most two months before Germany would launch a massive assault across the Channel, there was rising concern at Command and Establishment levels that the 109 was being seen as technically superior and a serious threat to our ability to defend the skies of the UK. Defeat of Britain was now seen by Germany as the main objective and the remaining obstacle to their grandiose plans for conquering the whole of Europe.

In the RAF the pilots of Fighter Command viewed all this with stalwart humour – 'That's what we are here for!' they said. But there was no widespread concern among them about 109 superiority; on the contrary we had great and appreciative confidence in our Hurricanes and of course the Spitfire pilots were totally convinced of their overall superiority as they still are today sixty years on, though not fully justifiably!

In the intervening years between 1940 and 2000, in an extraordinary roll of propaganda and ill-informed amateur speculation, the word has been spread that

Hurricane squadron in the Battle of Britain. The 'Vic 3s' drill was inflexible and changed later to the more efficient 'Finger-4s' of the Luftwaffe.

the Spitfire won every air battle and was the finest fighter of World War II without exception. But, although without question the most beautiful fighter design of all time and a delight to fly, it was certainly not technically 'the best' in all circumstances in the Battle of Britain or overall throughout the war.

In 1940 it was a match for the 109 at heights above 20,000ft and superior in performance to the Hurricane, but below 20,000ft the Hurricane was superior to both the others in manoeuvrability, gun-aiming, and ease of operation. However, these facts had not yet been established at the critical point that summer when a great air battle over the Channel and southern England was seen to be inevitable and imminent.

Providentially a Bf 109E, captured in April in France, had been repaired and tested by the French and then prepared for evaluation in this country. With my Hurricane squadron, No. 87, I was at 'readiness' one day in early May at Amiens Glisy when we had seen a small slim fighter come in to land, escorted by a Hurricane. The fighter had French markings overpainted on the originals on the fuselage and, we then perceived, a black and white 'swastika' still on its fin! This Bf 109E 'Werk nr. 1304', was soon on its way to AAEE Boscombe Down, where it was allocated RAF serial no. AE479 for what was now seen as a vitally urgent and important evaluation.

Boscombe Down's report was issued to the Air Ministry dated 10 June 1940 and contained the following extracts:

'. . . *All controls were effective, pleasantly light and "quick" up to 250mph, above which they became extremely heavy* . . .'

[compared to 350 for the Spitfire and 400 with the Hurricane]

'. . . *the elevator was out of harmony with the other controls and in the dive became almost immoveable* . . .'

[similar in the Spitfire, but not so with the Hurricane]

'... in aerobatics the 109 was impossible to loop in the normal manner due to heaviness and ineffectiveness of the elevator, flicking out over the top. Half-rolls off the top were difficult for the same reason ...'

[the Hurricane and Spitfire performing in both excellently]

'... Recovery from a dive was very difficult. In general the flying qualities were inferior [to the Hurricane and Spitfire] *at all speeds and conditions of flight.'*

Next, the 109 was assessed by RAE Farnborough with specific emphasis on comparative combat manoeuvrability as indicated in the following extracts:

'... as a fighter, the "Bf 109" was in general inferior to the Hurricane and Spitfire. [Its] heavy aileron control was not peculiar to the 109 [as] the early Spitfires suffered similarly [though not the Hurricanes] *urgent steps [are] being taken to improve Spitfires ...'*

'... Because of its highspeed stall a pull-out in a 109 near the ground could be dangerous ...'

'... When turning at high power both British fighters when flown by determined pilots could out-turn the 109 with its tendency to flick out of turn ...'

'... Perhaps the worst aspects of the Bf 109 (apart from its "snatching" slats, heavy ailerons and lack of rudder trimmer) were its uncomfortably "tight" cockpit and shortness of range ...'

'... In practice "dog fights" with Hurricanes and Spitfires, in the Bf 109E rapid manoeuvres at high speed were impossible due to control heaviness ...'

'... The 109E ranked about midway between the Hurricane and Spitfire in terms of top speed...'

The RAE report was dated September 1940 and issued to the Air Ministry (as an Aeronautical Research Council R&M) by the distinguished Farnborough 'Aeroflight' aerodynamic specialists M.B. (Morien) Morgan and D.E. (Dai) Morris, and both these sources have been available to, but seldom apparently referred to, by the historians and enthusiasts in the post-war years. However the Boscombe and Farnborough reports at that vital period in 1940 can be seen as definitive.

The roseate memories of the 'Spitfire boys' and their thousands of new-generation lobbyists will probably remain undeterred in their conviction that the 'Spitfire was the best'. But in truth in 1940 the 109, Hurricane and Spitfire were closely matched in terms of general combat capability. Each had advantages and disadvantages, and none had overall superiority.

So perhaps the surviving Luftwaffe pilot who appeared on TV at the Biggin Hill Battle of Britain air display in September 2000 should have the last word. He said: 'In this country you have it wrong. It was not the Spitfire which won the Battle in 1940 – it was the Hurricane!'

So what were the factors which resulted in the failure of the German air attack by mid-October 1940.

Firstly, it was not a victory or failure of aircraft quality contrary to the views expressed by many current historians (for example *The Battle* by Richard Overy, published in 2000, '... the Bf 109 was the world's best all round fighter in 1940 ...'). The opposing fighters were closely matched in combat capability, and the enemy bombers, dive bombers and *Zerstorer* low-attack fighters were formidable but not war-winning weapons on their own unless fully protected by their fighters, which did not prove to be achievable against the RAF.

'Rotol' prop. Hurricane of No. 87 Squadron on gun alignment. Exeter 1940.

Secondly, the fighting quality of the pilots and crews. In this major test of courage, determination and skills neither side showed advantage over the other. The RAF operated with the major tactical advantage of fighting over or not far from their home territory, with short distances to return to their bases for refuelling or forced landings; whereas the Luftwaffe had to operate from their French and Belgian bases, often over hundreds of miles of water on the way out and on the way back, and this also severely limited the fighters' 'time over target' because of fuel shortage. Then, in their long return flights damaged aircraft would often go down in the sea, unlike the RAF pilots who would most often be able to force-land in Kent, Sussex or further west and, if uninjured, return to their squadrons to continue the fight. So in terms of geography the RAF defending the homeland had this major advantage.

In the control of the battle there were two vital differences between the opponents: the command structure of the RAF was clear and decisive from the Commander-in-Chief Fighter Command, Hugh Dowding, through the AOC 11 Group (the main battle area) Keith Park, and the AOCs of 10 Group (West) and 12 Group (N.East) and this chain remained in place and operated with precision throughout the battle.

By contrast, the Luftwaffe 'KGs' and 'JGs', (*Kampfgeschwader* bomber groups and *Jagdgeschwader* fighter groups) were deployed from Brussels through to Cherbourg, and, though under the nominal control of their field commanders, were in fact under the dominance of Field Marshal Goering, Commander-in-Chief of the Luftwaffe, who often directed the day's battles personally from his command post on the cliffs near Calais. Frequently overriding his experienced professional staff officers, his orders were confusing and disruptive and many of his decisions and frequently directives from Chancellor Hitler himself, were misjudgements that had immediate adverse effects on their campaign. Examples of this were ordering the fighters into close escort with the bomber formations, which while it was enforced lost the fighters their vital flexibility and resulted in increasing losses to their bombers; and then at the vital and intense part of the fighting in August, ordering the cancellation of the effective low-level attacks on our radar chain and fighter airfields which were becoming a serious threat and which, if continued, might well have paralysed Fighter Command and altered the outcome entirely.

This policy change had resulted from Hitler's direct order at the end of August to concentrate all available forces in daylight attacks on London; and although this tactic did result in heavy losses and damage in the East End and Docks, it also, at a stroke, allowed the hard-pressed RAF to concentrate on one target area only, the approaches to Greater London from Dover and Margate. This made interception easier and gave more warning time as the massed formations crossed our coasts in only one area.

But possibly the most vital factor in our defence was radar. The 'Chain Home' (CH) radar defences, positioned in 1939 with brilliant foresight and planning around the coasts from north of the Thames estuary to as far west as Devon, was fully functioning in time for the battle; and through all the critical months from June to October our fighters were steered into accurate interceptions with very few failures, by the coastal radar stations which were able to 'see' and plot the courses of large and often even small enemy formations as they climbed up from the French coast towards Dover, Portsmouth, Southampton, Portland Bill or as far west as Plymouth. The information was passed instantly to the control centre at Bentley Priory, Stanmore, and simultaneously to the control centres ('ops rooms') at the headquarters of the relevant fighter groups.

By this means the traditional but wasteful 'standing' patrols were avoided and the squadrons held at readiness on the ground until the appropriate time to 'scramble' for the quickest possible intercept. At first the enemy could not understand how they were nearly always intercepted over the coast or even over the sea. Germany had no functioning radar system – theirs was still under development and would not be operational until 1941, so that all their fighter and bomber operations were dependent on desperately searching the skies for RAF fighters with, as we put it at the time, 'Mark 1 eyeballs'; while we were every day steered into visual contact with the enemy by the calm voices of our radio controllers, all themselves experienced pilots, with the constant updating of enemy positions on the WAAF-manned plotting tables in front of them. It was a masterly defence system and unique in the world at that time.

Much has been written and debated about the abilities and qualities of the opposing pilots in 1940 but there has never been any evidence of superiority of one air force over the other in this respect.

What is without question is that this was at the time the hardest fought air battle in history, and that in three unbroken months of fighting, often many times in one day, the fighter pilots fought with equal skills and tenacity. This demanded not only the instantaneous courage of the moment, but the continuous courage

Author with No. 87 Squadron in 1940.

to face battles every day until it was, or you were, finished. Both sides took this in their stride, to the great credit of their training systems and the quality of their pilots, and the degree of sustained courage and aggressiveness was outstanding in both air forces.

There was an imbalance in confidence at the beginning because there was no doubt that the Luftwaffe *Jagdflieger* (fighter pilots) were brimming with high morale following their successes, as they saw it, in the two previous air wars; the Spanish Civil war, and more recently the Battle of France in which they believed they had comprehensively beaten the RAF. But the latter, with typical Anglo Saxon stubborness and sangfroid, gained confidence in the successful fighting over the Channel in June and refused to be seriously impressed. They took the view that we had been outnumbered in France, but now from our own well organised bases and with all our marvellous supporting colleagues we were going to 'see off the Krauts' – no problem.

Well, it did not prove to be as easy as that, but at no time during that summer in which my squadron was continuously in the front line did we see any sign of

wavering. On the contrary their morale was so high and inspiring despite very heavy losses, that it inspires me still today. That determination and spirit was undiminished when, in October, it suddenly became apparent that someone was losing this battle and it wasn't us!

The surviving German fighter pilots have always maintained that they did not lose that battle, but that it was their high command and politicians who failed them, Goering and of course Hitler. The surviving Luftwaffe bomber crews were however greatly relieved to be withdrawn entirely from the daylight battle by the end of October.

So, the lessons to be learned?

British radar control was vital to the outcome of the battle, and because of this and the invincible determination of our fighter pilots and the quality of our aircraft, the Luftwaffe failed to destroy RAF Fighter Command or break our control over our Channel coast boundaries, and in trying incurred much higher losses than the RAF and could not continue to fight.

The RAF had beaten the Luftwaffe and

ABOVE: *No. 87's great squadron commander 'Johnny' Dewar DSO DFC.*

BELOW: *No. 87's stalwart ground crew. 'Blondie' Walton (left) was later injured in a bombing raid on Exeter airfield.*

No. 79 Squadron Hurricanes near Cardiff in 1941. CO and Flight Commanders Trevor Bryant Fenn, David Hayson and Roland Beamont.

won a historic victory. Consequently Germany could not launch its planned invasion of this country, and after five more violent years in the final outcome they lost the war to the forces of the combined Allied nations in 1945.

But the collapse of the Nazi empire, 'the Third Reich', began over England in 1940 and the victors were the Hurricanes and Spitfires and their pilots. (*See* Appendix 1.)

'Intruder'

An operation which led to a significant role change for a new fighter

A hard, white frost crunched in the grass under my feet as I walked out of the squadron dispersal hut towards my Typhoon. There had been low cloud with sleet most of the day, but now the frontal condition had moved out to the North Sea and a brilliant moon lit the huts and hangars of Manston snow-like in frost. It was close to midnight.

The Met. Office had said the frontal weather would still be over my planned destination, the Lille-Roubaix area in Northern France, and that the cloud base should be higher than it had been here, so I had decided to take a look. This was to be a solo experiment to investigate the offensive capabilities of this new fighter and was to attempt to confirm first impressions gained a few nights earlier in a moonlight sortie close to the coast of France near Abbeville in a successful attack on a leave train. As a result of this I had modifications carried out on my

The CO's Typhoon. PR-G at Manston.

Typhoon's gunsight and the front windscreen, in order to improve attack vision in darkness or dim moonlight; and now to test them and at the same time, hopefully, do some damage to the enemy.

PR-G's 'car-type' door and directly reflected gunsight - the 'local' modification.

Typhoon in No. 609's dispersal at Manston in 1943 (with the CO's car).

The other pilots were either still in our little Mess bar or sensibly in bed with 'Dawn Readiness' due in the morning. They were wondering what 'the boss' was up to. Weren't we supposed to be day fighter pilots? Well yes we were, but I was engaged in an interesting idea which, if it worked, would have a significant effect on the way the Typhoon could be used.

Since introduction into service a year before the Typhoon had proved difficult to clear for operations. Engine and airframe unreliability had given it a bad name with both pilots and engineers, and it had not proved capable of high-altitude combat operations. It was faster than any other contemporary fighter at lower and medium altitude however and had powerful armament and excellent control and stability, and I believed that it could become a significant and successful fighter in the 'tactical' ground-attack role.

I had recently received command of one of the first units with Typhoons, 609 'West Riding' Squadron, a famous Auxiliary squadron with a top-scoring record in the Battle of Britain on Spitfires, and finding at headquarters a general atmosphere of gloom and prejudice against the Typhoon I had requested an audience with my Group Commander, the AOC of 11 Group, AVM Hugh Saunders (later AM Sir Hugh). Much to my surprise and the astonishment of my immediate superiors this was granted immediately. The AOC listened to what this twenty-two-year-old squadron CO (of four weeks seniority in post) had got to say and then said, 'Well, what do you want to do about it Beamont?' Realising a hitherto closed door was being opened for me, I said that I was confident that the aircraft could provide for us the specialised ground attack capability which the air force did not have, and that all we needed to do was to prove it. I half expected to be 'shot down' but the great man said, 'Go on!' so I explained my plan to start by attacking transport targets; first by moonlight when the squadron was stood down from its 'day ops' commitment and then, if successful, by day in bad 'Rhubarb' style weather. Saunders twinkled and said, 'You know 609 can't expect to win this war all by itself, but I want to find out as much as possible about the Typhoon's potential. You can set up some operations and clear them with "Group Ops. Plans". Then come and tell me how you get on.' This was unprecedented, and for a short time I was conscious of criticism from some areas for jumping several layers of the command structure – I clearly hadn't been to Staff College, and some wing commanders and group captains were quite cross.

Back at Manston I put the plan into action with the guarded but enthusiastic co-operation of the senior NCOs who would have to provide some night service-ability in addition to our demanding daytime role, and when the word got round there was some concern among the pilots. The CO must be barking mad! But I had a plan for dealing with that.

And so as I approached my Typhoon PR-G white-frosted in the moonlight, I dismissed these secondary issues – that frost would have to come off the wings before it was safe to take off. But shadowy shapes with dancing lights showed where the flight-sergeant and ground crew were energetically brushing frost off the vital areas and clearing the windscreen and cockpit panels.

In the bitter cold they were dressed in their thin, unlined and ridiculously inad-equate uniform greatcoats, collars turned up against the wind around woollen balaclavas topped by forage caps at crazy angles, their hands only poorly pro-tected by short-fingered mittens.

Our forces were ill-equipped for what was expected of them in the early win-ters of World War II, and the pilots, who were no better protected, were thank-ful when they could climb into their cockpits and start their engines – at least they provided some warmth in winter weather. So it was on this occasion and by the time I had discussed the guns with the armourer and the new sighting arrange-ments with the flight-sergeant, and what I hoped to do with all of them, I was glad to close the Typhoon's incredible car-type cockpit doors and shut out the cold, but not before 'Good luck Sir,' came through the window.

Now was the moment of doubt; why was I doing this stupid operation? I could so easily be back in the warmth of the Mess with the others. But then the by-now routine actions took over. Engine starting and warming, checking all instruments, run-up to max. power and check magnetos. Then wave the chocks away and taxy out over the frosted grass past the waving torches of the ground staff who would then have to wait for a long two hours in the cold of their crew-hut for my return. All was concentration now. This operation might be difficult, but it was going to be interesting and it could be the beginning of something rather important. It was just up to me to get on with it – and come back with results!

Bumping out over the grass I noticed that the apparently clear moonlit sky was not so clear – the stars could not be seen below about forty degrees above the horizon. Signs of a mist forming, but that could be dealt with later. The immedi-ate interest was the weather on the other side. Dismissing all other thoughts I opened up the great thundering Sabre engine with little vision ahead of the engine cowling and glowing exhausts as we bumped over the rough grass. Gear-up and turning into the climb on course, any of the moonlit land below was soon

The No. 609 Squadron 'Intruders' at Manston in 1943. The CO (author) top centre.

lost. There was indeed a thick mist all round until we broke into the clear at about 10,000ft and settled into the cruise.

I was going to cross over the enemy coast between Calais and Mardyck in an area of no known heavy (88mm) flak and beyond the range of light defences, but after a few more minutes I could see a line of white cloud ahead. The front had not moved far away, and now I had to climb to 12,000ft to stay above the tops. After a further ten minutes cruise to take us well inland beyond the coastal defences, I checked time and gyrocompass heading, and trimming power back, began a steady descent into the cloud that would be continued down to the cloud base if practical, and into enemy country.

It was strange to be in this dimly red-lit, rattling and roaring box, with no visual cues coming in from the blackness outside to help in controlling our attitude, level or direction. This was going to go on until some outside reference was achieved at cloud break. But when would this happen, and would it be high enough to enable the operation underneath? This was always an act of faith in the absence of outside aids to navigation in fighters, or the radio altimeters, terrain-following radars and satellite-navigation systems of today.

But I was too busy to worry about the future just then. The altimeter unwound steadily to 2000, then 1000ft, and I checked the descent with still total darkness outside. If nothing appeared by 800ft I would have to level carefully at 700ft and open up smoothly back into a full power climb and go home. At about 800ft and still descending slowly there was a change outside. The pearl-grey mist all round began to change into darker patches and then, with a sudden sensation of speed, the dim shapes of woods and hedgerows disappearing underneath the nose very quickly.

At about 600ft we were clear of cloud and one or two dim lights showed where the blackout was not complete as indeed still happened in the UK, and now was the time to search for targets. Staying on the same heading which should bring us to the Lille area in a few minutes, the semi-darkness was suddenly split by chains of bright orange flak shells streaming towards us from the starboard side and then suddenly, it seemed, accelerating by very closely overhead to the accompaniment of the loud Woof–Woof–Woof of shockwaves. That was too close and there were now streaks of tracer fire from machine-guns coming from the same direction. Banking sharply away and diving even lower we left the flak behind, and I thought that it must have come from Lille Séclin airfield which had been ours in 1939/40 with 87 Squadron! But I could not see signs of an airfield and felt disinclined to turn back to identify it by the flak again!

So, still low down at about 250kt in the darkness, I turned north towards where I thought Roubaix should be and, suddenly against the dim ground ahead a patch or plume of white appeared. Turning to parallel it so as not to disturb it by my engine noise and cause it to cut off the tell-tale steam, I could clearly see its narrow source at one end and the thick trailing plume at the other, for it was a train moving fast. With insufficient light to see whether it was carrying passengers or freight, and as civil passenger trains were not legitimate targets, I set the gunsight, turned the gun button to fire and turned in for an attack on the engine itself squarely from the beam so as to avoid casualties on the train, and firing down to less than 100ft above it. The first burst of HE shells lit up a large locomotive with freight wagons behind, and then obliterated vision of it. Turning away I hoped not to lose it in the misty darkness, but after about 300 degrees of gingerly banking at this low altitude and without adequate visual references, there was the steam again but this time a big mushrooming cloud. The boiler had clearly been hit. I decided quickly to put another burst directly into the engine to ensure heavy damage and again saw in the fleeting light of the exploding cannon shells, steam gushing out along its full length. At this point there was a brief series of high-rate flashes which must have been from machine-guns or hand-held Schmeisser machine pistols, and then I was clear and climbing back to search again from 700–800ft.

Heading back towards the north the visibility began to improve, and in cloud-filtered light from the moon I could see about 1–2 miles ahead. It began to look as if I would reach the coast without seeing another target and then some indistinct lights appeared ahead. Losing some height but not aiming directly at them, I saw that there was a line of dim lights that seemed to blink intermittently. What I was looking at was a vehicle convoy moving along a straight road lined with trees which were momentarily cutting out the headlights as they passed. This could only be a military target and I turned the Typhoon round sharply in the much improved visibility and diving down, lined up for a firing run straight along the line of vehicles starting at the leader.

Firing a long burst obliterated the lights with explosions and smoke, and when I came round for another pass there was an angry red fire under the trees. I aimed another burst along the smoking line of targets, and this time received a short burst of machine-gunfire from the end of the column. This stopped under my

The author's Typhoon on the night 'Intruder' sorties from Manston in 1943.

cannon fire, and then my guns stopped – out of ammunition. After a further circle round the two fires now raging I pulled up, set climb power and climbed on my safety course, now in sleet or light snow, into the cloud base at 1000ft.

It was soon apparent that the weather system had changed because while there had been no icing in the cloud on the way over, ice now began to appear round the edges of the windscreen and out along the wing's leading edges. This would also be happening behind on the fin and tailplane which I could not see, and as it built up rapidly I began to wonder about carburettor icing. I didn't need engine trouble just now!

Still in cloud passing 10,000ft and with the windscreen apparently iced over, I increased to max. power to climb out as quickly as possible, and then at about 12,000ft broke into a moon and star-lit sky over a cloud sheet endless to the horizon. Settling down on course, I checked all instruments as the ice began to disperse in the dry air. The engine ran regularly (no Sabres could be said to run smoothly!) and this sortie seemed to be concluding satisfactorily, but there was more fun to come. The contrast of cruising in the empty night sky with what had gone on only a short time ago was remarkable and almost relaxing, but there was still important work to do.

At an estimated fifty miles from base and over the sea clear of the enemy coast, I called Manston for a bearing. They came back at once with a 'steer' and then confirmation that Manston was closed with fog! I was diverted to (code) Base, which I recognised as Bradwell Bay in Essex, and I was told that they also had fog but would 'get me down'. This was encouraging, and I knew that Bradwell were pioneering the new FIDO fog landing system, burning oil fuel in pipelines alongside the runway to disperse fog which I had seen in trial operation some time earlier. So I altered course a few degrees onto a new heading for Bradwell over continued pearl-grey mist, and calculated that it would take another fifteen minutes. The fuel gauges showed that this would be practical but rather tight.

So now at 9000ft and descending, I peered ahead for any signs of change in the white cloud or fog sheet. Then Bradwell called with a steer and said 'Main runway active, will steer you onto centre line'. They would not breach security by quoting the code 'FIDO' over the air. This was a rather interesting moment for it was to be a 'ground-controlled approach' for which neither I nor my pilots had been trained at that time, but now was as good a time as any! After one further 'steer' confirming my present heading they called, 'Turn port 40 degrees and descend to 500ft for final approach'. I did this, and when settled and descending towards what I could see was the tops of low fog ahead, I suddenly saw a change – there was an orange glow dead ahead in the fog. This got bigger quickly until the controller said, 'You are two miles from the runway, continue on this heading and descend to 300ft or until visual.' At that point the orange glow ahead split into two areas with a dark tunnel in the middle in which lines of smoky red fire on either side appeared, and then the runway with its lighting clear almost to its far end.

It was dramatic and miraculous, and quickly throttling back and flaring out, the Typhoon landed in the 'tunnel' safely and rolled, slowing down towards where an ATC vehicle appeared with a 'follow me' illuminated sign. And all around was smoke and fire with a clearly visible 'ceiling' of smoke and fog at only about 200ft above the runway. There was a moment when I wondered what would happen if I couldn't hold the Typhoon straight and drifted over the burning pipelines – it was clearly another hazard to be avoided.

At the station Mess I found a relieved crowd of pilots from many squadrons who had been diverted by fog to Bradwell and among them was Wing Commander Sammy Hoare, the highly successful and aggressive 'Intruder' pilot who specialised in deep penetrations over Germany to attack aircraft near their home bases. Sammy, with his famous 'handlebar' moustache, was waving a pint while loudly extolling the virtues of FIDO which he said was like Dante's inferno – he couldn't have got down without it and nor could any of us that night! Most of the stranded pilots were preparing to doss down in armchairs for the rest of the night, but I phoned Air Traffic and asked for Manston's weather – 'about 2000yd and 1200ft,' they said, 'and clearing.' So I returned to the airfield, started up the refuelled and still-warm PR-G and called for clearance onto the still smoky but adequately visible runway. This was given and with full throttle we were soon past the last of the flames and smoke and lights and climbing through the now shallow fog layer, back into the moonlight with a streak of dawn light lining the eastern horizon.

Manston was misty but the lights were visible and I was soon taxying in in the early dawn light towards waving torches which showed where 609's loyal ground crews were waiting for me after their all-night vigil. They crowded round as I climbed out, intensely anxious to hear how 'G' had done, then as I turned towards the Dispersal hut and the intelligence office and then eventually bed, one of them said, 'We thought we'd lost you this time Sir!' It had been an interesting night.

After about three hours' deep sleep I was up again to take 'Defaulters Parade' at the squadron office – my first time for this duty and I hoped very much for some guidance from our mature squadron warrant officer. This he duly provided

CO No. 609 WR Squadron at Manston in 1943.

The visit of the Air Minister to No. 609 Squadron, Manston in spring 1943. Left to right: G/Cpt Desmond Sheen, Station CO Manston, Sir Louis Greig, Air Ministry PRO, the author and Sir Archibald Sinclair.

with a sound but gently respectful manner. It was a great help, as indeed was the enthusiastic and continuing support I had at all levels in that great squadron.

Later that day in a call from Bradwell, the officer in charge of FIDO development said that 'last night was the first time the system had been operated in action and what did we think of it?' I told him that it had positively saved my aeroplane, possibly my life, and I congratulated him and thanked him. He then said, 'So said all the other pilots, and the night was a great encouragement to my team.' But although in limited use and always valuable throughout the rest of the war, the system was not developed or persisted with due to the very extravagant use of oil fuel which it demanded.

This sortie had provided the further proof needed. Typhoons could be used safely (relatively) and effectively in pinpoint ground-attacks in adverse, even severe weather conditions. More and more of our pilots were showing this as they volunteered to train at low level day and night and then began to plan and carry out their own solo attacks over 'the other side'. I had made it clear that these operations, which were extra-curricular and additional to our regular commitment of daylight Channel patrol against the prevailing 'Tip and Run Raiders', would be entirely voluntary. No one would be ordered to do them by me, although there might at any time be specific Form Ds from Group requiring ops. of this type in which the more practised we all were at this specialisation the better for each of us!

The idea caught on like wildfire (*see* Appendix 2), and by the end of the month all the pilots had volunteered and put themselves on my list for training. A number of the most experienced such as ebullient Norwegian Eric Hååbjorn, 'Pinkie' Stark, Remy Van Lierde (Belgian) and Jean De Selis (Belgian), had already started their 'private wars' and the squadron morale and enthusiasm for battle was heartwarming.

When my tour with 609 Squadron ended in May 1943 the squadron had achieved the highest score of 'Tip and Run Raider' victories (none of which had come my way when I was on frequent patrol which was frustrating) and in addition over 100 train and transport attacks on these voluntary operations. I handed over to ex-Battle of Britain pilot Alec Ingle who was told by AVM Saunders, '609 has very high morale and now you've got the difficult task of keeping it there.' Alec did so with elan and courage, further increasing 609 Squadron's prestige until he was shot down by an FW 190 and made a POW. Then his successor, Pat

No. 609 Squadron mess at Westgate in 1943.

Thornton Brown, carried on the tradition, taking it to new heights in new and varied operations involving deep penetrations of enemy skies in search of the Luftwaffe of whom they took considerable toll, and also 'ground targets of opportunity'. On the most famous of all, P.T.B. took 609 in company with 198 Squadron led by ex-609 member S/Ldr Johnny Baldwin, on a low-level 'search and destroy' mission over Holland, and arriving in the Eindhoven area by sheer coincidence during the arrival of a whole *Kampfgeschwader* (KG) of Dornier bombers from Germany for a raid on an English city that night, set about them and destroyed eleven 'for no loss, killing or wounding all the crews'. Some time later one of the KG's pilots who had been elsewhere on this day, was shot down over England and told his interrogators '. . . I thanked my lucky stars I was not flying that day . . .'.

In the early months of 1943 the successes of 609 Squadron in these difficult operations were of little significance in terms of damage to the enemy war effort, but they did what I had set out to do. The attitude 'get rid of the Typhoon' disappeared in the Service after a meeting was held at Fighter Command to which I was summoned and at which I was astonished to find the future of the Typhoon under review with cancellation in mind. After a long series of attacks, mainly by Spitfire-minded officers led, it seemed, by Chief Engineering Officer (CTO) Donald Findley who wanted cancellation of the whole Typhoon programme and purchase of a 'more suitable American fighter, the P47', which I did not consider suitable at all, I, as a twenty-two-year-old acting squadron leader was asked to say my piece in front of the Commander-in-Chief! Coming straight to the point, I said, 'Has anyone in this room flown a Typhoon?' (Excepting my colleague DeSoomer, CO of 3 Squadron, who was with me.) There was of course no response. Then, before anyone could argue the point I set out the actual experiences of 609 in the recent months and recommended the Typhoon as the primary ground-attack fighter for the RAF. The C-in-C then said that the matter could not be resolved at that meeting and would be reviewed. No more was ever heard of cancellation and in a major effort at the factories and in the newly forming squadrons with improved Typhoons, the massive and critically effective Typhoon ground-attack force was ready to support our armies in the invasion of Normandy in 1944. There, by the end of July, they were brilliantly successful in destroying the Panzer armies at Mortain and Falaise, facilitating the break-out from the British and Canadian sector and across the Seine and leading to the advance through France, Belgium and Holland, and ultimately to victory with our Allies in Germany. In all of this the Typhoon ground-attack force was the critical factor in hitting hard-point resistance ahead of our ground forces, and they were held in highest esteem by the soldiers one of whom wrote to me, 'Thank God for the RAF Typhoons in 1944 – we would have been lost without you'.

Very many brave Typhoon pilots were lost in that intense fighting, and their efforts and the magnificent support of their ground crews in the dangers and hardships of the battle for Germany played an immensely valuable part in the final victory. Those lonely solo Typhoon ventures in the winter of 1942 had proved worthwhile. (*See* Appendices 3, 4 and 5.)

Hitler's flying bomb attack on London – politics behind the Battle

The third of these stories took place during the last great battle for London in World War II, and in the following account there were some strange events

In February 1944 I had been tasked by the AOC of No. 11 Group Fighter Command, AM Sir Hugh Saunders, to form No. 150 Wing, the first with the new Hawker Tempest fighters and, after training-up, to position them at RAF Newchurch on Dungeness to prepare to provide fighter cover over the coming Normandy Invasion and if it became necessary to switch at minimal notice to defending London against an imminent mass attack by Germany's 'secret weapon', the Fieseler Fi 103 V1 flying bomb, the Tempest being the fastest fighter available for this critical task.

Working-up operations in May over France and the Low Countries had gone well and then on 'D-Day', the Invasion of Normandy on 6 June, my Tempests had patrolled the massed shipping lanes and the Invasion beaches.

A Hawker Tempest VI at Hawker's Langley factory in 1945.

On 8 June, 'D+3', my Tempests encountered Bf 109 G6s attempting to penetrate the left flank of the Invasion area and we shot down three of them near Rouen without loss. No. 150 Wing was getting into its giant stride and then on 15 June Newchurch was brought to immediate 'Readiness' for Operation 'Diver Alert'. The expected Flying Bomb attack had started.

Although as the Wing leader I had known of this possible commitment for over three months during which I had expected and had endeavoured to obtain without success, technical and operational details of this threat in order to plan interception methods and tactics, nothing had been divulged at all. But at dawn on the morning of 16 June my Tempests were ordered off on 'standing patrols' along the Channel coast until further notice together with the advice that 'a wave of attacks by V1s is in progress coming in between Beachy Head and, North Foreland, target London'. That was all.

I asked 11 Group's operations planners for information on the plotted height and speed of the raiders, and the voice said, 'About 2000ft but no other information. You'll have to go and find out!'

In doing this we soon established interception techniques which enhanced the basic radar instructions and enabled us to progress on a steep learning curve.

Newchurch destroyed eleven V1s on the first day and had achieved 100 by the end of the first week. This was a significantly higher success rate than any of the other fighter units, and an order of magnitude improvement on the initial performance of AA command whose thinly dispersed gunsites and outdated manually directed 3.7 guns and relatively ineffective Bofors had them struggling to get into even double figures each week in June and early July.

As a result of the Newchurch success rate (*see* Appendix 6) I was summoned to report to 11 Group with recommendations, and I asked for immediate banning over Kent and Sussex of the widespread 'free-lancing' of the slower fighters from other sectors, as these were actively interfering with the dedicated defence

The author, Wing Leader of No. 150 Tempest Wing during March to September 1944 (Tempest VN751/R.B.)

A No. 3 Squadron Tempest at Newchurch in 1944, with a patrol returning from flying-bomb operations. (Note the protective cover on the Tempest's 'clear-view' canopy.)

squadrons and were achieving few successes in their enthusiastic but misdirected and unco-ordinated activities.

I also called for the AA guns to be concentrated on a narrow coastal gun-belt, and for the fastest fighters, the selected squadrons of Tempests, Spitfire XIVs and Mustangs, to be instructed to intercept over the Channel or between a new concentrated 'gun-belt' and the London 'balloon belt' so as to avoid the fighters being shot at by our guns – as was now frequently happening with inevitable casualties.

Thirdly, I asked for Observer Corps units to be spaced at equi-distances around the coast from where they could fire signal rockets towards any V1s sighted. The converging smoke trails of any two rockets would then help the fighters' initial sightings.

These measures were all implemented in July with consequent improvements in success rate.

But other factors were emerging in what was now a crisis scene, for London was coming under truly massive assault by waves of hundreds of V1s at a time with the fighters destroying 925 in the first month, but guns and balloons only 312.

At the very beginning of the attack I had been surprised to receive a tersely worded signal from the headquarters of ADGB (Air Defence of Great Britain), which had overall responsibility for this battle although the fighters (mine included) were directly controlled by Fighter Command's 11 Group Sector which included Kent and Sussex.

The signal stated that 'pilots were not to claim destructions of flying bombs as "Victories" as having no pilots the V1s could not be compared,' it said, 'with the destruction of a manned aircraft.'

This seemed to me to be a strange instruction to give to pilots who were facing a vitally important and most probably hazardous operation; and who would in any case be the last to claim undue credit for what they would not expect to be a thankless task.

But on reflection I was not convinced of the logic of this comparison between an 'unmanned' flying bomb and a 'manned' aircraft.

Were not RAF and Allied fighters frequently credited with 'victories' over Europe against Arado and Bucker trainers, Me 108 and Caudron Goeland light transports and Ju 52 troop transports, all of the Luftwaffe and all of which were completely defenceless, whereas the Fiesler V1 flying bomb carried 1800lb of Amatol high explosive which could and often did bring down the attacking fighter as the bomb exploded under the fighter's cannon fire.

But being rather busy with fighting the battle, after passing on this message from on high I dismissed it as of no consequence though rumblings in the squadrons continued for some time to indicate that this particular appreciation of their efforts from the headquarters of ADGB was regarded by them as surreal as

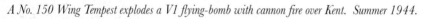

A No. 150 Wing Tempest explodes a V1 flying-bomb with cannon fire over Kent. Summer 1944.

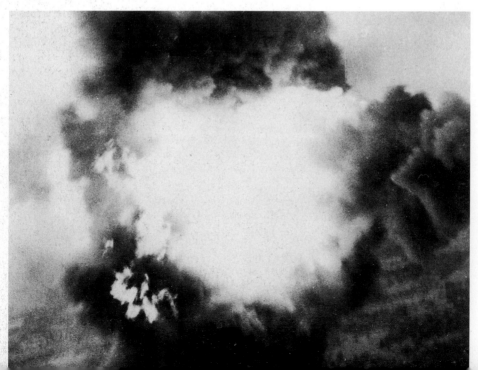

Bob Cole of No. 3 Squadron (21 Flying Bombs destroyed) looks at his Tempest's rudder, burnt by an exploding V1.

their casualties mounted, and out of touch with the real world of the fighting line.

No fighter pilot that I ever spoke to would ever have wished to claim a V1 as a 'victory', but they would and did record it in their log-books as a 'destroyed' with my full and continued support.

Meantime our casualties from wild AA gunfire missing V1s but hitting our Tempests continued to mount; fighters were brought crashing down in full view of the people of Kent and Sussex and there were headlines in the press and questions in parliament.

I was not surprised to learn that AA Command were becoming embarrassed by this adverse publicity, but I was astonished to be instructed to go to their area headquarters at Hastings 'to make peace with them'! Since it was my pilots who were being killed I rather felt that the boot should be on the other foot, but when I went with my colleague Newchurch Commandant W/Cdr 'Digger' Aitkin to dine at the AA/HQ Mess, I found a sea of brown backs in their ante-room and a universally hostile atmosphere broken only by a radiant young girl lieutenant who took me into dinner!

I was introduced to General Pile, Commander-in-Chief of AA Command, who was scarcely civil and hoped that the RAF would discontinue their complaints. I had not made any of course to the press or to sources outside formal reporting channels, and so I said that I hoped that the cause of any complaints would be removed by his gunners being persuaded not to fire at our fighters. This did not improve the atmosphere and I left as soon as etiquette permitted.

The results of Newchurch's learning curve were dramatic with 200 V1s destroyed by 29 June, 300 by 7 July, and 500 by 26 July. In the first month fighters destroyed 925 and the guns of AA Command totalled 261.

It was an immense and sustained effort by all flying and ground personnel day and night without rest or leave. Individual pilots were each flying three to four sorties a day and often some at night, and on many occasions destroying two or more V1s in a single sortie.

In the middle of all this pressure Johnny Iremonger, CO of 486 Squadron, came in to our tented Mess one evening and said, 'Did you see Sir Roderick Hill (Commander-in-Chief, ADGB), he was here today flying one of my Tempests.' I said no, I hadn't known of the visit, and Johnny said, 'Well, I didn't notify you, Sir because I assumed you knew!'

This was surprising. Roderick Hill was our overall ADGB Commander and, if he had wanted to fly one of my Tempests normal protocol and courtesy should have ensured that his staff notified the Wing Commander Flying!

Once again I was too busy to pursue this irregularity, but I could not help noticing later in the regular intelligence summaries from ADGB and Air Ministry press hand-outs, frequent references to the C-in-C/ADGB's periodic sorties in 'his Tempest from Kenley to destroy V1s' in which he was not apparently successful.

With the successes of the fighters mounting higher every week there continued to be other voices apparently unsympathetic to our efforts.

Certain Spitfire leaders were heard to say that 'true fighter pilots' should not be employed in shooting down flying bombs, but they should be reserved for the 'pure and glorious' activity of one-to-one air combat! But these voices did not feel it necessary to mention that their Spitfires had been found wanting against the V1s (except for the latest and relatively few Mk XIVs) compared to the Tempests, and that all the Spitfire Mk Vs and Mk IXs had been withdrawn from this vital battle for London because they were too slow! The smell of sour grapes was in the air.

Then in early July I was summoned at very short notice, together with exuberant American Buck Feldman of 3 Squadron, to attend a Field Investiture (*see* Appendices 7 and 7A) at Hartford Bridge Flats (today's Blackbushe Airport). After flying my Tempest RB to Lasham next day and shooting down a V1 near Hastings on the way, we received our 'Immediate Awards' from King George VI and afterwards I had the immense pleasure with Shirley, my wife of only a few brief months, of meeting and talking with Queen Elizabeth whose wonderful charm was as great then as it is today fifty-five years on.

Unusually, there had been no prior citations or other information on these awards, but when I was able to read the *London Gazette* five days later it referred to '(The author) having formed and led a fine fighting unit'. Well, I agreed that this described the Newchurch Wing well, but it seemed odd that there was no reference at all to the V1 battle.

We still had the battle for London on our hands however. Losses and injuries to pilots mounted and the Wing's score of V1s destroyed had reached over 600 by mid-August. The main defence of London against them was concluded by the end of August when the mass attack reduced to a trickle as the British Army overran most of the enemy launching sites in their advance through France and Belgium; and then another strange phenomenon occurred.

It had been rumoured throughout the summer that there was conflict in high places in the Services over the conduct of the V1 defensive operation which was indeed a critical battle for London, and General Sir Frederick Pile, C-in-C of AA Command, is recorded as having written a memorandum in September 1944 including the remarkable statement:

> 'There was no doubt in my mind which needed the greater courage – to stand on a gunsite and fire at a directly approaching flying bomb with the knowledge that it will hit you if you bring it down, or to fly an aircraft at a suitable distance behind the bomb and shoot it down. Any pilot who shot down a large number of V1s could count on receiving yet another decoration . . .'
>
> (Longmate, Norman *The Doodle Bugs*. Hutchinson)

The unfortunate fighter pilots shot down by General Pile's gunners or brought down by exploding V1s would not, of course, be so rewarded.

This unseemly observation was then followed almost unbelievably by Prime Minister Churchill in a memo to the Chiefs of Staff RAF:

> 'You have no grounds to claim the RAF frustrated the attacks by V weapons – so far as the flying bombs were concerned the RAF took their part but in my opinion their efforts rank defnitely below that of the AA Artillery . . .'
>
> (*Aeronautical Review* (June 1990). Putnams)

This at the very time in September 1944 when the official statistics of the battle for London from June to September showed: Balloons 231, Guns 1460, Fighters 1772.

That is to say that, in this crucial defence of London, fighters destroyed more VIs than all the other defences put together! (*See* Appendices 8 and 8A.)

The Newchurch Tempest Wing alone destroyed 638, which was more than one third of the total shot down by all the fighters. Warm acknowledgement of their efforts was received from No. 11 Group Headquarters and also from Sir Ernest Gowers, Regional Defence Commissioner for London on behalf of London's Town Clerks. But nothing at all was heard directly from HQs ADGB.

I wondered why.

Following the end of hostilities in 1945 and some brief but interesting interludes in the immediately post-war RAF, my war-service on the Reserve ended and a turning point arose.

In February 1946 I was offered a Permanent Commission in the Service which I loved, but just at that point opportunities were appearing in which I felt that my acquired knowledge and skills in test-flying could be usefully applied in the new and exciting introduction into aviation of 'jet' engine power. A whole new generation of aircraft designs was in sight in a major step forward in aviation technology.

It was an inspiring prospect but a hard decision to take with our fast-growing and increasing family foremost in our minds, and my wife Pat (we had married in 1946) in her calm and supportive way said, 'We must do what you think best'.

She knew what the answer would be and it was most probably not the one she would have chosen. But as always we laughed at the difficult ones and she said, 'If you stay in the RAF you'll become an Air Marshal ... like all our friends – and I'd be an awful Air Marshal's wife,' which was certainly not true!

So, after some further early jet experience at Gloster's and de Havilland's I joined a company little known in the aircraft industry in 1947, English Electric near Blackpool in the North-west.

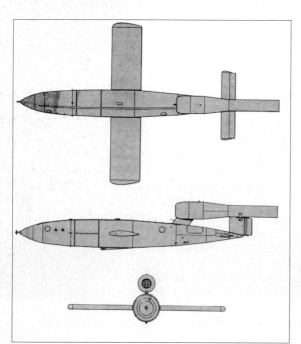

The Fieseler Fi 103 (V-1).

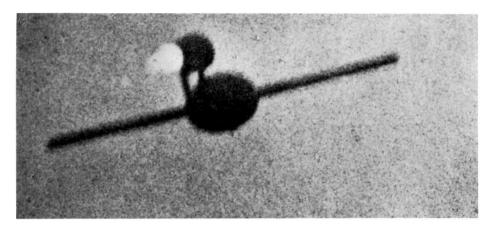

A V-1 as seen by an attacking pilot.

The author, leader of 122 Tempest Wing 2nd TAF, and S/Ldr 'Digger' Cotes Preedy, CO of No. 3 Squadron in Brussels during September 1944.

CHAPTER TWO

ENGLISH ELECTRIC AVIATION
– A BRITISH SUCCESS STORY

A personal view of thirty fascinating years at Warton with Britain's leading
military aircraft manufacturer

In the years 1949–79, Warton produced under its successive reorganisation titles EEC, BAC, and BAe (nationalised and de-nationalised), six major new military aircraft types of which five were supersonic and twenty major type-variants; and this family led to the successful 'agile' supersonic fighter technology demonstrator, the Warton EAP of 1980, and to its major successor the international Eurofighter/Typhoon of the 1990s and beyond.

In this timescale the total production of military jets for the RAF and many of the world's air forces up to 1999 had been over 3000 aircraft; while in addition over 500 Warton designs had been built for overseas air forces under licence.

In parallel to all this activity, the English Electric Lightning won the intense international competition in 1965 to form the basis for a supersonic defence system for Saudi Arabia, and this immensely valuable export programme has been running continuously ever since and now, under the title 'Al Yamamah', has been officially recorded as 'Britain's most valuable single export programme' over more than thirty years.

This unique history has culminated in the development of Warton and Samlesbury today (1999) as the main centre of British military aircraft design, development and production, and after more than twenty years of the successful Tornado programme Warton is now approaching the production phase of the Eurofighter/Typhoon which promises a twenty-year programme for at least 1000 production aircraft.

A story of continuous success over forty years broken only by the BAC TSR2 saga which was a failure of government and the procurement system and in no way a failure of Warton's technical excellence (in partnership with Vickers); the TSR2 in fact demonstrating in its short period of flight testing that it was more than likely to have been able to achieve the advanced military capability targets set for it.

This Warton story began in the last months of World War II when the late Lord Nelson of Stafford with great foresight formed an entirely new design team at his English Electric facility at Preston in order to undertake Air Ministry specification B3/45 for the future (and first British) jet bomber for the RAF.

This was at the beginning of the era of the 'new jets' when work was already advanced in this country on two jet fighters, the Vampire and the Meteor, and specifications were being drawn up for three four-engined jet bombers, the

Post-war de Havilland Vampire production at Samlesbury.

Valiant, Vulcan and Victor.

These three were all ambitious swept-wing designs and as a fall-back insurance against the risk of failure of this, for the time, very advanced programme, a more conventional straight-winged four-jet design was also ordered from Short Bros. and named 'Sperrin' together with a smaller twin-jet bomber aimed as a replacement for the famous but now outdated Mosquito.

It was a period of great movement in aviation – the race was on for the airforces of the world to become jet powered!

At English Electric there was a sound background of aircraft engineering experience gained in the successful licensed production of many hundreds of Handley Page Hampdens and four-engined Halifaxes which had been Preston's most valuable contribution to the war effort between 1939 and 1945, and now post-war they were diversifying into Vampire jet fighters under sub-contract to de Havilland.

This was providing a major step forward at the Preston and Samlesbury factories in engineering experience on high-performance jet aircraft, but until 1945 there had been no aircraft design capability at Preston since the earlier World War I activity, which had ended in 1921.

The entirely new team recruited and set up by newly-appointed chief designer W. E.W. 'Teddy' Petter specifically to undertake the twin-jet design, was not given much chance of succeeding, in what was seen as a very major task, by the rest of our aviation industry many of whose leaders would dearly have liked this contract and who almost universally regarded English Electric as 'inexperienced interlopers in the North'!

This view was deliberately lobbied throughout the corridors of the Air Ministry and Ministry of Aviation for many years and did nothing to help the emerging 'newcomer'; and this influence was indeed still evident even in the 1960s when the contract for TSR2, at that time the world's most advanced strike aircraft, was granted to the firm in the newly-formed consortium which had a total absence of experience in the design, development testing and operations of supersonic aircraft – experience which already existed in abundance at English Electric!

This was one of the factors, perhaps the most vital one, which led to the ultimate failure of that programme.

But in 1946 the new Preston team were largely young and enthusiastic about the 'new jet bomber' they would be designing, and they had all been prepared to take a chance in exchanging relatively secure posts in the old established companies in the South for what many felt was an uncertain future at Preston.

I was one of these and was the last to be selected by Petter for his 'senior staff', with the title of 'Chief Test pilot'.

In 1946 I declined a permanent commission with the RAF with some reluctance in order to join the industry at the exciting time of the 'jet revolution'. I had already done some test flying with Gloster's and de Havilland's and had then decided to approach English Electric. When I arrived for interview and walked down the cold rain-glistening and virtually derelict Corporation Street from my over-night stay in the then execrable 'Vic and Station' hotel – in which my cell-like bedroom had been, it seemed, all night in the middle of the Preston Station marshalling yard – the general atmosphere of gloom was not improved as I turned into the EEC design offices that had been set up as a temporary measure in a deserted pre-war garage, Barton Motors, which had been a training centre during the war hence the title 'TC'.

Once inside the dilapidated building a hive of activity was apparent in a row of metal and glass partitioned offices on the second floor, all of which looked over what had been a spacious car service area and was now almost filled with an impressive-looking wood and cardboard mock-up of a sleek twin-engined jet.

My interview with W. E. W. Petter was impersonal and brief and I was told to nominate a referee 'who would know something of my character and experience'.

I could think of quite a few, but told Petter that I would think about it and write to him. He seemed surprised at this and said, 'Well, make it soon,' and the visit to Lancashire and my possible future workplace ended there!

I did not anticipate a problem in finding someone, but it needed the right choice as I had a family to support and an apparently secure post at Hatfield that should not be put in jeopardy for a risky move which was what my friends lost no time in suggesting that Preston would be!

I had served under such fine commanders as Sir Hugh Saunders of 11 Group and Sir Harry Broadhurst of 2nd TAF, and for a period Philip Lucas, chief test pilot of Hawker's, all of whom would I felt sure have taken a supportive view of my proposal to take on the test flying of the RAF's first jet bomber, but there was another man with what seemed to me to be a unique background.

As C-in-C/ADGB (Air Defence of Great Britain) Sir Roderick Hill had been my overall commander in 1944 when my Newchurch wing had been top scorer of all the fighter Wings against the V1 flying bombs. He had also been a distinguished test pilot himself at Farnborough between the Wars, and was undoubtedly aware that my tour in 1943 at Hawker's in the final testing of the new Tempest had led to my being charged with forming the first Wing of these fine new fighters in time for the Normandy invasion in1944; and he would have known of the success of that Wing.

It did not occur to me until much later that the stiff and formal level of communication (or lack of it) between the staff of ADGB and their operational squadrons, which I had experienced in 1944 and which had contrasted strangely with the close and warm 'operational' support that we were used to from 'Dingbat' Saunders' 11 Group, might in fact have originated with their distinguished commander himself.

So I wrote to him and soon after received his invitation to lunch. This took place at the Waldorf Hotel in London's Aldwych. It was an odd event and left the impression of a certain lack of enthusiasm on Roderick Hill's part, although he was of course polite.

I heard nothing more for three months and began to wonder what had gone amiss, and then in March 1947 a letter arrived from Petter with a date for another interview.

This time he was more welcoming and said, 'Well, there has been some debate about the appointment – you have been short-listed with S/Ldr Tony Martindale, (an experienced and courageous RAE test pilot with an engineering degree which I had not!) but it has been decided on balance that we have plenty of good engineers and what we need is a pilot with both operational and test flying experience – so do you want the job?'

After a brief discussion of terms of employment which included a salary equivalent to my recent RAF rank of Wing Commander I agreed, and no mention was made of Roderick Hill so I assumed he had been supportive.

Some forty years later, after my retirement I was shown a letter which had emerged from the Warton files dated 1946 from Roderick Hill to Teddy Petter saying: '. . .Beamont had some effective operational experience but I doubt if he has the technical qualifications or ability which you require.' It was fortunate for me that Teddy Petter, advised by Freddy Page, had made his own judgment which launched me on a career which lasted for thirty-two fascinating years at Warton and included test programme responsibility for five major new-type jets, four of them supersonic, and sixteen new type-variants.

The years 1948 and '49 at Preston were at once inspirational, frustrating and worrying.

The task of the design team to produce a twin-jet light bomber with world-beating performance against a tight timescale focussed minds without need for any encouragement, which was just as well in view of the meagre financial rewards at that time.

But relationships between the 'newcomers from the South' design team and traditional Lancashire production engineering 'works' had become a serious management problem, with designers receiving little or no co-operation in their contacts with the Strand Road Works whose managers frequently expressed themselves bluntly about 'that bunch of Southerners at Corporation Street'; and there emerged another source of frustration.

Inmates of the Air Ministry OR (Operational Requirements) Branch and of the MAP (Ministry of Aircraft Production) clearly did not relish their necessarily frequent rail safaris 'up North' to the often dark, wet and gloomy Preston to attend and often to chair technical and contract progress meetings, and they did not help the general atmosphere by all-too-frequently expressing their view that 'English Electric will have to learn how to conduct meetings' – this was generally in response to determined refusal by the Corporation Street team to be deflected from their professional intentions in this important contract by junior civil servants who, in their opinion, did not know what they were talking about!

This all led to some nervousness about the future. The jet bomber was an inspiring and demanding target, but would its achievement be possible in an atmosphere of doubt and carping criticism from the officials from London, and in spite of continued stubborn lack of co-operation from the production works?

In this continuing situation the concerns at Corporation Street became less confused and more clearly defined. The difficulties on all sides had to be faced and resolved and the new design made a resounding success for without this the new English Electric design office would clearly fail and be closed down and the team would be out of work; and this would happen within two years or at the most three.

So this was the dilemma faced by the Chief Engineer, Teddy Petter, who had not only to lead the technical drive but had to overcome the prejudice on all sides which threatened to undermine the programme.

This prejudice even emerged in Flight Operations! Shortly after joining the company in May 1947 and becoming involved at once in work on the B3/45 mock-up cockpit, it became apparent that nothing was being said about the Vampire production test-flying programme at Samlesbury and when I asked about this Petter said, 'You'd better ask Sheffield about that'. Arthur Sheffield was the redoubtable and much respected Works Manager of English Electric Co. (Preston and Samlesbury) and would, I understood, be responsible for Vampire production and for building the B3/45 prototype, so I asked to see him.

He was standing behind his paper-strewn desk in his large office in the Strand Road Works when I entered and at first impression he seemed spare, wiry and nervous-looking, but when he spoke he was direct and uncompromising, brushing aside my introductory offerings.

'What do you want?' he said. I said that I understood that there were production Vampires on test at Samlesbury and when would he like me to take charge (I was employed as Chief Test Pilot) and start flying.

With no hesitation he said, 'You are bloody Petter's pilot. You'll not fly my bloody Vampires,' and showed me the door.

This presented a number of problems, but on the way back to 'TC' I reflected that this was not a tenable position for Sheffield, for Petter or for me and that it would probably resolve itself.

Sheffield's Vampire back-log at Samlesbury was I knew building up, and 'his pilot' Johnny Squier could not cope with all of them.

Reporting to Petter, he was not surprised and said 'Leave it for a few days and see what happens.'

But next day the telephone in my small office rang and a voice said, 'Walker 'ere, when are you coming to fly my bloody Vampires!' I said, 'When Mr Sheffield authorises me to take charge as CTP.'

George Walker, Superintendent of Samlesbury Flight Shed, said, 'You'll have to ask Mr Sheffield.' I said that I already had, and after a few fruity Lancashire expressions Walker rang off.

Next day he rang again and said, 'You'd better come down and start flying. Mr Sheffield says it's alright.'

So I went to Samlesbury where I found that it had been left to me to explain to the resident pilot Johnny Squier that he was no longer in charge. He was understandably not overjoyed to hear this, and he took some time to accept it before settling down in the new regime for a long career of distinguished production and experimental testing at Samlesbury and Warton.

But it all started off, as George Walker elegantly put it, as a 'booger's muddle'!

Throughout 1947 the new design progressed well despite the working complications, and while it became clear that the design office operation and the production works organisation would have to develop an ability to work together despite the mutual at-loggerheads of their principal managers, one alleviating feature emerged.

One of Petter's major targets was for his own experimental and prototype assembly shop; an idea which was totally dismissed by Sheffield who had set up an 'experimental department' within his Strand Road Production Works in which he intended that the prototype should be built.

But the shop was now in the charge of Bob Hollock, an experienced experimental engineer who had been recruited from Vickers at Weybridge, and who had his own brand of belligerent independence that enabled him to take full advantage of the continued dissention between his design and production bosses!

Thus the Corporation Street (TC) designers found that they could monitor the build process of the prototype directly with Hollock who was only too happy to carry on without reference to Sheffield 'as long as no-one interfered with the way I want to built it!'

I soon found that the design office had some formidably independent thinkers on their own account and, in addition to the severe and eccentric brilliance of Petter who made it penetratingly clear that he was totally in charge, Don Crowe with responsibility for systems and production standards, Ray Creasey the genius of Warton's aerodynamics, and Dai Ellis flight development and designer of Warton's and Britain's first supersonic wind tunnel, were the leaders of an enthusiastic and capable team who were not about to be deflected from their current major task but were already considering the next stage of 'English Electric Aviation' which, in their view, should be a supersonic fighter with sufficient performance to intercept their own bomber, 'because nobody else is building one!'

With this far-sighted idea in mind Petter asked for my views on the possible merits of carrying out flight research into stability and control at the highest feasible combinations of altitude and Mach No., and I said that my recent experience at Gloster's had shown that they had not investigated 'compressibility' on their Meteors above 35,000ft, and nor, I believed, had the RAF.

I suggested therefore that a Meteor IV could produce some valuable information from 35,000 up to about 47,000ft which was its practical manoeuvre ceiling.

Petter thought so too, and with enthusiastic support from the Air Ministry he apparently had little difficulty in obtaining a Meteor from the Ministry of Aircraft Production on contract for thirty hours of high Mach No. research.

I collected Meteor IV serial EE545 from the Gloster test airfield Moreton Valence on 6 August 1947 and headed for Warton, leaving behind some rather puzzled Gloster flight test people who wondered what was going on!

Some time after this I received a peremptory letter from Bill Waterton, the newly-appointed Chief Test Pilot at Gloster's, demanding to know what 'English Electric thought they were going to do with a Meteor IV that Gloster's had not already done!'

I reminded him politely that as senior experimental test pilot there until recently I knew what Gloster's had done, and more to the point had not done with their Meteors, and that we proposed to fill in the gap in their high altitude 'compressibility' knowledge.

This began an interesting programme of flights during the winter of 1947–48. All of these involved ceiling climbs above 45,000ft and were conducted in unavoidably primitive trial conditions.

Warton aerodrome had been deserted for many months following the post-war withdrawal of the USAF's major maintenance base. There was no air traffic control and base security was covered by one 'Works' policeman on a bicycle.

The Meteor was supported by three ground staff, a fitter, a rigger and a tractor driver, and this team was run by 'ground staff foreman' Bill Eaves who also deputised as air traffic controller. When he had supervised engine starts and cleared 'chocks-away', he then proceeded onto the airfield with an Aldis lamp (borrowed by the author from the RAF) and signalled Reds or Greens to the Meteor as appropriate prior to take-off and landing.

With no nav-aids or ground-control radio, each flight was a free climb, generally to the north-west over the Irish Sea reaching 45–47,000ft near Douglas, Isle of Man, and then the Meteor was rolled over to dive back on a reciprocal heading in the direction of Warton and the onset of buffet, wing-drop and finally nose-down loss of control was noted in the range of 0.79–0.83 Mach. Sometimes this would be exceeded in out-of-control 'compressibility' dives until control could be regained by closing throttles and extending air-brakes (which had a useful nose-up pitching moment) and recovering to level flight around 30,000ft or lower.

From this position the recovery to Warton was often 'blind' without nav-aids through thick cloud, and in the winter months heavy icing frequently occurred on the outside and inside of the cold-soaked and at that time unprotected front windscreen panels.

Often this obscured all forward vision and then steps had to be taken to melt off the ice by 'ram-temperature rise' at speeds above 400kt IAS at low level.

By then the pilot needed to know where he was, as the fuel state would be low after all that full-throttle work!

This programme was very successful and Petter reported his findings to the Ministries, concluding that contemporary fighters would have no curve-of-pursuit intercept capability against B3/45 (Canberra) type performance above 30,000ft, and would even have difficulty at that height (as was ultimately proved at the first Boscombe Down trials of the Canberra in 1949).

The B1 serial VN799, in 25 Hangar at Warton before its roll-out in May 1949.

This report was received with great interest in Whitehall and at RAE and resulted in letters of congratulations on this work, the Controller of Aircraft, John Boothman, saying that the matter was of great interest and asking if Petter had any objection to the report being circulated in the RAF!

Petter of course had no objection and followed this up with a paper recommending that to intercept an aircraft of Canberra-type performance at 40,000ft and above, a fighter with supersonic performance and manoeuvre capability would be essential and that Warton design studies, a copy of which he enclosed, had shown conclusively that this could be done and that English Electric could do it!

By early spring 1949 the Canberra prototype, VN799, had been moved to 25 shed at Warton for final assembly and systems testing with no major problems arising. As the first flight approached the spirit of eager confidence that had become widespread at Warton was modified, at least in the flight test area, by a sober appreciation that this was no run-of-the-mill 'latest prototype' but rather the first public revelation of the yet-to-be-proved skills and professionalism of the Warton team. Much depended on the outcome for all involved, and this attitude had led to a cautious approach to the initial testing.

At my suggestion it was planned that after ground handling for steering and braking had been extended to response to elevator at nosewheel-lift speed, some short straight flights would be flown if practical to assess response to controls and

The author with the first prototype B1 (Canberra) VN799 at Warton in May 1949.

stability before full committal to flight.

With a main runway length of only 1900yd at that time these requirements sounded somewhat ambitious to some people, but at the planned very low fuel state and with a fixed flap setting of 30 degrees for max. lift the performance estimates indicated that the aircraft could take off at about 80kt in 700yd, fly level for up to 500yd and have 700yd left for the landing run providing speed was held precisely down to a maximum of 90kt, and also providing that the wheel-brakes energy absorption capacity proved adequate. But precise flying would be needed.

During the work-up taxying on 8 May careful brake temperature measurements were made at progressive speeds, and ultimately a max. brake slow-down from 100kt proved a clear margin of safety temperatures for the 'hop' tests.

I had by then gained strong confidence in the general 'feel' of the prototype which I described in de-briefing as 'taut and high quality'; and so it was decided to go ahead.

The first 'hop' on 9 May went exactly as planned enabling assessment to be made of elevator in rotation to lift-off, in throttled-back level flight and in flare-out to a gentle touchdown with throttles closed; and the landing roll was comfortably stopped with 200yd of runway to spare.

Second and third hops to 15ft and 500yd on 9 and 12 May demonstrated

Canberra B1 VN799 on Flight 1 at Warton on 13 May 1949. The only in-flight photograph showing the original 'tall' rudder shape which was changed for Flight 2.

aileron and rudder effectiveness, and so the way was clear for Flight 1 with a high degree of confidence as I had already landed the aircraft three times!

Much has been written about the Canberra's first test flights and the outstanding debut at Farnborough 1949, and the subsequent testing and development of Britain's first jet bomber. Sufficient to say that in the next twenty years seventeen air forces world-wide found it superior to any other twin jet of its time.

The Royal Air Force operated eight variants of the Canberra, and the PR9 version was still giving fine squadron service in the year 2000 with more years to come; the first aircraft type to serve in the RAF continuously for fifty years!

Some problems were encountered in the early development years as there always are in aircraft testing programmes, but the Canberra has gone down in aviation history as being remarkable for high reliability, ease of maintenance, exceptional manoeuvrability and role flexibility in its success in world-wide operations, and for the confidence and enjoyment of its pilots. It has always been a pleasure to fly a Canberra!

Britain's first jet bomber in July 1949 at Warton.

The author flying the English Electric B1 Canberra prototype, approaches the camera located in the tail turret of a Lancaster in June 1949. The photograph shows the extreme manoeuvrability of the Canberra in only its first month of testing. (No zoom lens.)

CHAPTER THREE

'FOUR-BREASTED BOILER'

Not long after I joined EEC a very interesting opportunity arose. The Ministry of Supply told Teddy Petter that prior to my beginning the B3/45 testing they wished to send me to the States to obtain some experience on the newly-emerging American jet bomber prototypes such as the Martin XB48 (four engines, straight wing), North American XB45 (four engines, straight wing), and the Boeing XB47 (four engines and 35° swept wings and tail surfaces).

Since these were all in initial prototype testing and classified highly secret, I thought this programme very ambitious to say the least. However Air Vice-Marshal Cuckney, the 'Deputy Controller Aircraft', was positive about it implying that without this experience I might not be granted 'approval to test' the B3/45 series; and I was anxious to proceed so plans were made.

Meantime Cuckney then came up with another consideration. The Americans were now apparently saying that before flying their jets the British pilot must be able to show evidence of heavy four-engine experience!

I was basically a fighter pilot and at that point 'current' on Vampires and Meteors which did not really meet the requirement and so the AVM, in no way to be frustrated said, 'Beamont must do a Lincoln conversion!'

To do this, and also for the American tour, I had apparently to be seen as an RAF officer, so I was recalled on the RAFO (Reserve of Air Force Officers) and told to wear uniform in my substantive reserve rank of squadron leader.

But time was pressing and since my uniform carried the 'retired' rank of wing commander I asked if that would do, and the reply was affirmative!

Presenting myself at RAF Wyton, the station commander was puzzled but helpful and introduced me to a young flight lieutenant who was to be my instructor.

The latter eyed my uniform with its World War II medal ribbons and said, 'I thought you were a civilian'. I explained my temporary situation and he said, 'Well, with all that lot you ought to still be in the Service!' and then as an afterthought, 'Sir!'

The following morning the Wyton tarmac was crowded with huge four-engined bombers – Lincolns – and with no prior ground briefing I was shown round one before climbing up into the high cockpit of this vast 'four-breasted boiler', as the four-engined bombers were impolitely known in Fighter Command.

A thorough briefing followed conducted by the flight lieutenant and an attentive NCO flight engineer who was to be the other crew member.

Then I set about learning to fly an aircraft by numbers! This was apparently a normal procedure in Bomber Command but it was entirely new to me and slightly unsettling.

Power settings for take-off. 'Rotation' speed, climb at 180kt to 800ft after u/c and flaps up.

Port turn 90°. 2 min. at trimmed power for 180kt.

Port turn 90°. 3½ min. at trimmed power for 180kt.

Port turn 90°. On to base leg for 2 min. U/c down. Flaps down. Trimmed power.

Port turn 90°. On to finals. (Pick up glide slope indicators.)

Power to fine pitch and throttles trimmed to 175kt on the Approach slope.

(No viewing of the airfield until it appears straight ahead!)

Flare over threshold markings and throttle back progressively until wheels touch, tail high.

Ease wheel back progressively until tail-wheel contact and then concentrate with rudders and brakes to prevent weather-cocking, especially when subsequently taxying back across- or down-wind.

Throughout all this I had been positively discouraged from looking for the airfield or visual turning points, being told merely that 'You will see the runway when you turn finals'.

On the downwind leg there had been time to consider this great aeroplane with its massive Griffon engines grinding and rasping out on the wings on each side. The control forces were seriously heavy and I was at once reminded of Sir Frederick Handley Page's famous quote, 'You can make a barn door fly if you put big enough engines on it' – I think he must have had the Lincoln in mind!

I also noted the firm stability on all axes and realised that this quality would have been essential for the courageous bomber crews on their night-long sorties on instruments over Germany in generally atrocious weather in their Lancasters and Halifaxes. We then did another circuit in the same routine and when taxying back near the control tower I noted a line of airmen on parade and wondered what they were there for.

An Avro Lincoln from RAF Wyton, as flown by the author in 1948.

At that point my instructor said, 'OK, off you go for one circuit just like that. The flight-engineer will look after the engines and systems,' and then he disappeared down the ladder!

I started a conversation with the engineer who seemed quite happy at the prospect of accompanying my first solo on the Lincoln (I doubt if he had another option!) and then something else unexpected happened. Up the ladder and disappearing into the bowels of the Lincoln came that long line of airmen! I questioned this and the engineer said, 'Oh yes, the airmen can volunteer for air-experience flights and we take them as often as we can.'

At that point I wondered whether there would be a sudden exodus down the ladder if they were told that their pilot had not flown a Lincoln solo before!

But we were soon thundering off down the runway flying the 'numbers' again without reference to our position relative to Wyton or anywhere else in Cambridgeshire for that matter, until, with a distinct feeling of pleasure the runway appeared ahead as we turned from base leg onto finals!

The landing was quite presentable. The airmen trooped off happily (some actually thanking me!) and after thanking my mentor I was able to record in my log-book, 'Lincoln conversion. 1½hr dual. 30min. command.'

This was duly authorised by the station commander, but with some amusement as a full operational conversion would have been a very different matter, and I returned to Warton with a 'four-engine qualification' and heightened respect for the stalwarts of Bomber Command whose normal task was the driving of these vast, cumbersome vehicles thousands of miles through all weathers.

In the event my subsequent visit to the USA in May 1948 proved both frustrating and fascinating. The two big jet bomber prototypes were on prolonged ground testing and were not available for me to fly, but the smaller North American B45 second prototype was flown twice from Muroc in the Californian Mojave desert, and it was an interesting aeroplane.

A medium-sized four-engined type with conventional 'straight' wings and all-round powered flying controls, it was fast and easy to fly low down but it rapidly ran out of performance and manoeuvrability above 25,000ft, which limited its load-over-distance capability severely. I felt it might have a useful though limited reconnaissance role but that was all, and that it would prove inferior in all respects to our forthcoming English Electric B3/45.

But then I had an opportunity, also at Muroc, to fly 'one flight only' in the second prototype N-A XP86 Sabre jet fighter which was under development for the USAF.

In a fascinating flight I reached more than Mach 1 in a comfortably controlled dive, becoming the fourth pilot to do so (and the first British pilot to reach Mach 1) and then at low altitude a speed exceeding that of the current official world air-speed record. It was obvious that this was a magnificent aircraft with formidable fighter potential. The long-awaited breakthrough to practical supersonic flight was there, and my report back to English Electric and to the Ministry and Service authorities was received with serious attention and also scepticism in some quarters for a while in London and Farnborough until it finally sank in. The Americans had produced the world's first practical transonic fighter which was so advanced that two squadrons (of F86 Sabres) were eventually procured for the RAF in the NATO Front Line in Europe as we would have nothing to match them until the Hawker Hunter which was under development and still some years away from Service entry.

A Lincoln from RAF Binbrook visits Warton with Bomber Command crews to see the first four Canberra B2s in 1950.

CHAPTER FOUR

TESTING BRITAIN'S
FIRST JET BOMBER

1949 was the threshold of a new era in aviation, an era in which the performance of large aircraft, military and civil, was more than doubled overnight in a technical advance unprecedented in the first fifty years of aircraft design and development.

With the steady but relatively slow evolution of piston-engine power from the 1920s up to and during World War II, the performance of new-type aircraft world-wide had increased only modestly at around 50mph per decade, and by 1945 with the by-then available larger 2000hp engines, fighters were for the first time exceeding 440mph and bombers and transports 300mph.

Then the introduction of practical gas turbine 'jet' engines resulted in 1945 in entry into service of the first jet fighters with speeds approaching 600mph.

But the big piston-engined bombers, Lincolns, Boeing B29s and Liberators, and the Douglas and Boeing airliners in service, were still in the 300mph plus category when the British and American industries launched the first practical multi-jet designs which were going to be very much faster.

In America in 1948 there emerged a number of four-engined prototypes and in Britain one twin-engined replacement for the Mosquito, and later the three heavy 'Vee Bombers'.

The first British venture was the English Electric B1, later to be named Canberra, and it was regarded as something of an enigma.

It was twin-engined and small in comparison with the other contenders, and there were wide-spreading rumours that it was likely to have greater performance than any of the other new bombers. These were scoffed at, but not for long!

At English Electric the design team working on this inspiring project had grown accustomed to the knowledge that 'if it all works' their jet bomber would be able to exceed 600mph, 50,000ft and 2000 miles range in just its initial form, and that there was much potential for future development.

These speeds and altitudes were clearly in excess of what was expected of the American jets and in personal experience of one of them, the North American B45, I had confirmed its maximum speed of about 520mph and a maximum practical operating altitude of little more than 30,000ft. It was not going to be in the same class as the Canberra!

So in the spring of 1949 as the B1 neared readiness for flight, a wide range of opinions were being expressed on its probable future.

At the Strand Road, Preston, Works of English Electric there was an atmosphere of clearly expressed doubt as to what 'that carnival lot at Warton' (the design team) were capable of, and whether their product would ever provide a production run for the 'Works' to carry on with from the end of their current sub-contract on Vampires for de Havilland.

At Warton the small number of designers and specialist engineers who had worked for this day for five stressful years were now facing their moment of truth. They had immense confidence in their professional skills and pride in what they believed they had achieved, but was the B1 too great a step forward? A bomber with twice the speed of most of its predecessors and faster than any of their replacements and designed by a team which had not worked together on any project before, was clearly being regarded elsewhere as a high-risk-venture; so had they got anything wrong? These thoughts were in many minds at that time, but they were never allowed to reach the hearing of the flight test team who went about their final preparations with professional calm and eager anticipation, but probably also with some reservations of their own about how it would all turn out!

Away from this centre of activity there was a different atmosphere. In many offices in Whitehall and the research establishments there was continued outspoken criticism of the English Electric B3/45 programme along the lines of, 'Why are we building a small twin-engined aircraft when what is required is a four-engined bomber in the Lancaster and Lincoln tradition?'

And then the fundamental issue: 'Why has the design and development of the first British jet bomber been placed on a little-known heavy-traction manufacturing company which has never designed a modern aircraft before? This of course was the theme widely promoted and lobbied by many of the old-established aircraft manufacturers who, now running out of contracts after the war, would dearly have loved the 'jet-bomber' work and considered that it should have been theirs by right!

So that when the all-blue painted English Electric prototype VN799 was rolled out in May 1949 from its decrepit and run-down ex-wartime hangar on the near-derelict aerodrome at Warton on the edge of the river Ribble near St Annes-on-Sea which was to be its base for test flying, there was an air of expectancy and rising enthusiasm. This was a beautiful aircraft indeed!

The trials began in an atmosphere of calm and professional planning, for although the team was entirely new and on its very first prototype programme it had been working on the project for four years and each individual member had had prior specialist experience at other companies or research establishments. There was no hint of amateurism and the work proceeded with confident expertise. When problems arose in the final preparations for flight as they always do, there was someone there on the spot with the answer.

At this stage I became aware that a new phase had been reached in which the specialist engineers were no longer taking arbitrary decisions themselves to finally sign-off items for flight, but were now tending more often to confer with the pilot before doing so.

This was fundamental in building team confidence in that the engineers were glad to have the pilot involved in sharing 'operational' decisions, and the pilot gained confidence from the knowledge that the engineers were confiding in him.

This was by no means universal practice at that time or even always at Warton in the future, but it resulted in a great feeling of confidence on the day.

At 9 a.m. on Friday 13 May 1949 the principal engineers and chiefs of the inspection departments were gathered in Petter's office together with the Chief Test Pilot (the author) to review the final clearance documentation when Petter turned to me and said, 'Friday the thirteenth is not everyone's idea of a good day for a first flight. If you want to postpone until tomorrow I would agree with that.'

I said, 'The weather is right. The aeroplane is fine. Let's go flying!' And so we did at 11 a.m. that morning.

What followed was a remarkable event that set a new milestone in aviation and affected the lives of many thousands of people in the aircraft industry and air forces around the world.

The first flight of the Canberra proved also to be a turning point in my life. Since leaving school I had enjoyed the proud privilege of my seven years in the RAF in which I had seldom had to search for action – it had always been there to deal with in the company of magnificent and heart-warming colleagues who had set the highest standards to follow.

Then, in the aftermath of war with Pat and the children to be cared for, I had been able to use my acquired test flying experience to gain interesting posts in the aircraft industry culminating in chief test pilot of English Electric. It had seemed attractive work that would keep a roof over our heads and, with luck, pay school fees in the future. But now the job had changed scale.

In this flight on 13 May I very soon became aware that this was no humdrum conventional aeroplane with merely increased performance over its predecessors, but that it was an altogether new and different experience.

As the prototype lifted off the Warton runway responding smoothly to elevator, I selected the undercarriage UP immediately – we had not at that time become alerted to the possibility of systems failure of the type which occurred many years later in the first flights of another new and more complex type!

The wheels retracted into the wings with satisfying thuds and the sequence lights went out; now for progressive investigation of trim, stability and response to controls.

But already there was a difference. I was not having to closely co-ordinate the climb path as the B1 was continuing on its own undeviating climb with no help needed from me!

It was as if it was on auto-pilot although none was fitted, and I quickly looked more clearly at this aspect.

Even throttled to climb power speed was increasing rapidly and needed reducing to stay within the limits set for this flight, and now it was quite clear that this aeroplane had an unusual degree of steady symmetry in its flight path. Response to elevator and aileron was smooth and precise and no re-trimming had been necessary.

In stability checks it was apparent that the short period damping was 'dead beat' on all axes when climbing at 220kt, and then when checking the rudder more positively there was a yawing lurch, the rudder pedal-force gradient seemed to almost disappear and then the rudder required positive pedal force to return it to neutral.

Calling to Johnny Squier to observe this from his Vampire, I repeated the action with the same lurching yaw resulting.

Johnny could see nothing unusual but this had implications of inadequate control for crosswind landings and, more importantly, in controllability in the event of a single engine failure.

I felt that we were experiencing rudder over-balance and decided reluctantly to return to base.

By this time at 10,000ft and at a low power setting to stay at 220kt IAS there was an almost unreal quiet in the cockpit. Little airflow noise was apparent around the smooth nose and one-piece semi-spherical Perspex canopy, and engine noise was apparent only as a low background hum. Radio reception from Warton Tower was outstandingly clear when I notified them and Johnny Squier of my intention to return for a trial approach and possibly a landing off it.

Reducing power further to begin the descent immediately showed low drag, and I soon had to throttle back to 'idling' in order to achieve an adequate rate of descent at this speed.

On the downwind leg I lowered the undercarriage with no problems, and then the flaps which produced a pronounced nose-up trim change that I found could be trimmed out, but only just, by full 'nose-down' tailplane trim. A point that would require attention.

Now turning base leg over the Ribble Marsh sewage farm to line up on long finals for Warton's 26 runway it was already clear that this was a very unusual aeroplane. It virtually flew itself, needing only the gentlest indications from the pilot of the required flight path.

There was a surprising sense of security in this aeroplane after only twenty minutes of its first-ever flight, and it was necessary to remember firmly that there was in fact a discrepancy with the rudder which could at any time cause a difficulty!

At about this time, and while gently rolling out of the final turn and making only small throttle adjustments to approach speed, a sudden bounce of turbulence from the fields below (it was a hot sunny morning) caused a slight yaw which, with instant rudder correction, immediately resulted in the 'over balance' lurching disturbance again.

This was quickly stabilised by returning rudder firmly to neutral, and the approach continued slightly higher and faster than intended following the distraction.

But over the boundary and crossing the runway threshold the aeroplane felt in such perfect control with safe margins in all critical areas that I continued to flare easily and precisely over the runway 'Numbers' and held off, floating as the speed decayed, and touched down gently about 400yd down the runway with 1500yd ahead in which to slow down smoothly with gentle braking and running dead true down the centre line.

The flight had lasted only twenty minutes but it was already clear that this was a very exceptional aeroplane, and we had not even begun to look at its potential performance and manoeuvrability!

I taxied 799 back to the west end of Warton's long tarmac to the small waiting group – no 'reception committee' but just the people who had seen me off, the crew chief Jimmy Pickthall and his ground crew and Bob Hollock, the experimental manager. Petter had decreed that no other personnel would leave their work places and that de-briefing would be in his office.

I walked across the tarmac, telling Hollock that we had a good aeroplane with little that needed immediate attention.

In the office Petter headed the long table with the original briefing group of specialists round it all looking I thought rather tense, as if wondering why the flight had been cut short.

I did not let them off the hook immediately but went straight into a progressive account of the details of the flight, confirming acceptability or otherwise of each point until I came to the rudder incident which I described carefully.

Saying that I believed this to be rudder over-balance with flight safety implications for crosswinds and engine-out control, I said that this would need resolution before flying again.

Immediately there was a reaction from one of the engineers that 'it couldn't possibly be overbalance!' But Petter said, 'It quite possibly was and no-one should jump to hasty conclusions.'

In continuing to describe the flight I gradually lightened the atmosphere by telling them of all the good points, and I concluded by saying that I was sure that we had an absolute winner here and that it was 'fit to fly again now if it wasn't for the rudder'.

I was aware that conservatively cautious engineers would tend to factor a relieved test pilot's euphoria so I did not reveal at that stage what my true reaction was, that in my ten years of flying, wartime and testing, I had never experienced such qualities before.

This had been only a few minutes in the beginning of the exploration of a potential flight envelope far in excess of any other modern design, and so there could well be many problems and even major ones ahead. But for now I was sure that the English Electric B1 was going to be a brilliant aeroplane, and I had the amazing fortune to be the pilot!

Next followed a private discussion with Petter in which he analysed my reporting stage by stage, not allowing himself any signs of enthusiasm until he finally said, 'Well, what do you think of it?'

I said that I had been trying to find fault with my first impressions but I couldn't, and that I felt we had got the basis of a very fine aeroplane indeed.

Petter allowed himself a small smile and said he thought so too but now was a time for everyone to control their enthusiasm professionally, or words to that effect.

He then called a meeting of specialists around 799 in the hangar and looking at the tall, rounded rudder, said, 'Well, that's what we made the top in wood construction for, so that it can be modified quickly if required!'

Ray Creasey of aerodynamics and some of the structures engineers discussed with me again the effects of the overbalance I had experienced, and then talked to Petter about the amount and shaping of the rudder horn balance area that might be effective.

Decisively Petter told Creasey to issue dimensions to the design office for a modification to the rudder, and the programme was begun at once.

The prototype was rolled out with an interim 'new shape' to the rudder and prepared to fly again on 18 May, and on this flight which I approached with eager anticipation, I found that the modification had eliminated the rudder problem. The aeroplane now handled smoothly and conventionally in yaw, and it was tested out to 420kt IAS and climbed to 14,000ft, all in the smooth conditions of Flight 1.

Now we began to notice something else of great importance. This very new and very advanced aeroplane refused to become unserviceable in the normal fashion of a new type.

It was just inspected, refuelled and turned round post-flight, and after the third flight (on 19 May) the rate of testing increased rapidly until, with accumulated modifications to incorporate, 799 laid up after Flight 11 on 11 June.

Some elevator 'flutter' had been encountered so the elevator horns and mass balances were altered while the final 'production standard' rudder-horn modification was done, and then testing was resumed on 8 July.

From this date to 31 August no fewer than thirty-six test flights were made covering the whole initial design 'flight envelope' including climbs to above 40,000ft and clearance of the initial RAF requirement of 470kt IAS.

The prototype continued to fly superbly, and with authority to show it at the coming Farnborough air display in September I began to think about putting a demonstration sequence together.

On 22 August, after completing a compressibility investigation to Mach 0.82 in level flight at the Tropopause in which I had found the onset of mild buffeting but no loss of stability or reduction in flying control effectiveness, I throttled back and entered a smooth and quiet descent to 10,000ft and then began to look at aerobatic manoeuvres. This was an odd thing to be doing in a bomber aircraft, but with its relatively low wing-loading and the excess power available from these impressive new and easy-handling Rolls-Royce RA2 Avon engines it seemed likely that aerobatic manoeuvres could be achieved safely and without difficulty. Nevertheless it was with a conscious thought that if anything did go amiss blame would fall squarely on me for unscheduled and unauthorised flying that I began a cautious investigation at 10,000ft.

First setting up 300kt IAS I banked thirty degrees to port and then rolled up smoothly to forty-five degrees into a full aileron roll to starboard maintaining positive G in a 'barrel' roll. This 'bomber' rolled smoothly round through 390 degrees where I corrected to wings level. No height had been lost in the roll and the small amount of yaw developed had been easily corrected with rudder. It had felt like a beautiful roll and a natural manoeuvre for the aeroplane!

After repeating this with increasing enjoyment a couple of times, I trimmed into a shallow dive at 400kt at 7000ft and pulled smoothly up to the vertical before throttling back and kicking hard right rudder into a semi-stall turn, watching for any effect on the engines and pulling smoothly out of the following dive but with quite heavy wheel-force to level back at 7000ft.

These pull-out forces would need watching, but it was all so trouble-free that I went straight into a half-loop and 'roll off the top', using 400kt at the pull up and barrel rolling out cleanly at the top at about 180kt. This bomber could have been designed for aerobatics!

So now to complete the exercise and assess the height needed for a full loop. Beginning this at about 420kt at 7000ft the Canberra went easily over the top at 190kt and about 10,000ft with sustained and quite heavy pull-force that was eased off over the top until diving vertically again, and then pulled strongly out but well with the 5G limitation to level again at around 7000ft.

This suggested that with experience full loops would be possible for lower speeds and within about 3000ft of airspace. This aeroplane could most certainly be used for low-level display flying!

I throttled back and pointed the Canberra in from the Irish Sea over the coast at Fleetwood in the direction of Warton, quietly gliding and minding its own business in the way that was so characteristic of it, and on the way back I began to consider how this aerobatic capability could be worked up to include the tight-turning manoeuvrability potential with its low wing-loading and general ease of control. It all looked very promising.

So at the end of the next test flight on 23 August, with a fuel state close to the load we would plan for a Farnborough display, and at low level over the sea off Barrow I looked at turning capability with increasing enthusiasm. The Canberra would go round in a near-vertically banked turn at 250kt and 2.5G in what seemed to be an exceptionally small radius, and so I carefully increased G at this speed until the first sign of the stall boundary buffet appeared as a mild vibration. This occurred at 4.5G and was clearly not the final limit, but this could not be safely assessed at low-altitude so I went up to 5000ft to repeat it and pull to the limit.

I had of course investigated the 1G stall in earlier flights and it had been innocuous with a mild wing-drop quickly recovered with slight forward wheel, so I did not expect the accelerated stall to be a problem.

Again at 250kt in a nearly vertical bank I saw 4.5G as before at the buffet onset, and then 4.75G with heavying buffet before 'departure' rolling away to starboard and immediately controlled with forward wheel.

Returning to the Warton circuit I put this manoeuvre into perspective by breaking left from the 26 runway line at about 200ft and pulling a 360 degree turn at 200kt that went round completely inside the aerodrome boundary, and was certainly noticed by those watching!

This confirmed my feeling that something unusual could be done at Farnborough that could be entirely safe but which would most probably not be matched by any other aircraft there.

At this stage voices began to say that a valuable prototype bomber should not be risked in aerobatics, and I was careful to restrict further practice to well out of sight of Warton. In the meantime, Teddy Petter, who of course had a major interest in the outcome, merely said 'The flying department will know best how to present the aircraft at Farnborough,' and he left it to me entirely.

I flew 799 down to Farnborough late on the Sunday for opening day. With no further practice (at that period no time was allowed for this at Farnborough), when I taxied out and lined up for the Canberra's first public display no-one knew what to expect of it and the general view seemed to be that it was an inter-esting-looking twin-jet but that, as it had not got the currently much sought-after 'swept' wings, nothing much new was expected of it. It just, they said, looked like a rather large Meteor!

But it did not behave like a Meteor and its six minute sequence of tight manoeuvres in the vertical and horizontal, nearly all within the perimeter of Farnborough Aerodrome, was something which had not been seen ever before in a bomber design. This caught the imagination of the aviation press and the atten-tion of the aviation establishments in this country and abroad, and before long our intensive test programme suffered frequent interruptions for demonstrations to prospective customers such as the United States Air Force, and at major over-seas air displays such as Paris and Antwerp where at the latter the Belgian Press described the Canberra as 'the Hero of Antwerp'!

After the 1949 Farnborough debut the Canberra programme took off. By November the trials had progressed so well that I took the prototype to Boscombe Down for a 'Service Preview', and at that centre of traditional scepticism where the RAF test pilots' views were 'don't trust anything the Industry says', their report on the Canberra was unanimously enthusiastic, one of the senior pilots

The Canberra's first Farnborough Show on 6 September 1949.

799 begins its take-off run on Farnborough opening day.

Britain's first jet bomber, the Canberra, taking off from Farnborough on 6 September 1949. (Author)

Canberra B2 prototype VX165 at Farnborough in 1951 flying over the mighty Bristol Brabazon.

The author flying the Canberra T4 prototype at Farnborough in 1953. Rudder, elevator and ailerons all at full travel just after take-off at an altitude of only 30ft.

saying in his report, 'it is the finest aircraft I have ever flown'.

The development programme was soon into the standard B Mk 2 for the RAF, the T4 trainer, the PR3 and PR7, the Mk 5 prototype and Mk Bi6, then in 1954 the Bi8 and the final main variant in 1958, the PR9 which is still in service in the year 2000 and is to be finally phased out in 2005. Over fifty years of service.

Chapter Five

A British bomber for America

In August 1950 some signals were received at Warton indicating American interest in this new English Electric multi-role twin jet and on 18 August I flew the prototype VN799 from Warton to the nearby USAF base, Burtonwood, to give a demonstration to a party of American air force generals.

The weather was bad with low cloud and rain, but this suited the exceptional characteristics of the Canberra which could manoeuvre tightly in these conditions, pulling off spectacular vapour vortices from its wing-tips in what was described as a dramatic display.

The generals, we heard, were impressed and very soon we were notified that a USAF mission would arrive at Warton 'to evaluate the Canberra for possible acquisition by the USAF'!

There was immediate reaction of amazement, and then expressions of serious reserve at 'Establishment' levels where the whole suggestion was apparently regarded as 'seriously premature – the Canberra has not yet even been accepted by the RAF!'

Despite all this, being Americans they came anyway and as Chief Test Pilot I prepared to receive and brief the mission leader, the redoubtable Col Albert (Al) Boyd, chief of the USAF Flight Test Centre at Wright Pattison AFB whom I had met there in my visit to evaluate American jets in 1948. He had severely rebuked me for bursting the nosewheel tyre on one of his P80 Shooting Stars!

Al Boyd stated his requirement for six planned sorties covering the flight envelope which had been suggested in our briefing, and that he would fly each sortie first, which would then be repeated by the two other test pilots in his team. He would not report his findings to us but would return to the States in five days to make his report. We would receive a copy in due course.

Meanwhile his engineers would sit with ours and study the design and the status of the flight testing and development programme.

This sounded satisfactory to us, as we were very confident in the unique qualities of the aircraft and in the rate of progress in its testing and I had great respect for Al Boyd.

As in the case of the first (and very successful) RAF trials of the prototype at Boscombe Down recently I offered to fly with Boyd, sitting on the 'jump-seat' beside him as there was no dual-control, and he said 'Not necessary. Just give me the numbers.'

It was an approach I appreciated as it indicated his confidence in my briefing and in his ability to decide precisely how he intended to proceed. There was nothing indecisive about Al Boyd!

These trials were completed in six sorties over two days with the Canberra being ready as required each time, and after discussion on how the design could

The author demonstrating Canberra B2 WD932 to the Martin Company at Baltimore in 1953.

be readily transferred to USA if a procurement under licence to build in that country should be required was met with our answer that the Warton design system of 'loft-plating' would be readily adaptable to shipping the total design by air at quite short notice, the colonel and his team departed without showing obvious enthusiasm but also without showing any professional criticism. Knowing Al Boyd I took this to be an encouraging sign.

The design loft plates were airlifted in USAF DC-4 transports directly to the Martin Co. plant at Baltimore in 1951, after I had demonstrated B Mk 2 serial WD932 to Pentagon officials in a 'fly-off' competition at Andrews Air Force Base, Washington which we won hands down; and a programme to build a Canberra series in America modified to USAF requirements, rapidly gained momentum.

In 1953 I took part in the initial trials of the first US conversion, the Martin B57A, and also of the B57B, the final configuration of the Martin-built Canberra, and I found little difference in the handling and performance characteristics when compared with the British Canberra.

However the B57B version had a completely redesigned nose, and the controls and systems layout in the new tandem cockpit were in many ways improvements

Canberra B2 WD932 at Martin Airport Baltimore, for the fly-off competition on 26 February 1951 at Andrews AFB Washington.

The main competitor (which lost out to the Canberra), the Martin XB51 - WD932, in the background.

on our original, as was their vastly improved weapons system.

In performance aspects there was no improvement and the compressibility (Mach) limits were slightly down on those of the Canberra B Mk 2.

But the Martin Co. had made some extravagant claims about carrying out 'significant' aerodynamic improvements, and this was highlighted at a briefing given at the Martin Middle River Airport for test pilots of the USAF Wright Field Test Centre.

Martin's redoubtable Chief Test Pilot, Pat Tibbs, concluded his enthusiastic presentation by saying, 'and finally gentlemen the performance of the Martin B57 bears absolutely no resemblance to that of the English Electric Canberra'!

From the back of the hall I said, 'Quite right Pat – it's worse,' and the meeting broke up in laughter.

The Martin Co. built over 400 Canberra B57s and variants for the USAF, in whose capable hands they became the most effective 'night intruder' aircraft in the Vietnam War.

There were many testing milestones in the establishing of the Canberra's remarkable record and one of the most memorable of these occurred in 1952.

At that time the USAF had already established their programme with the Glen L. Martin company of Baltimore to build over 400 Canberras under licence as B57s for the USAF and two British Canberra B2s had been delivered as 'pattern' aircraft to Martins, the first by an RAF crew in 1951 and the second by the author with R. H. T. Rylands, radio operator, and D. A. 'Watty' Watson navigator, on 31 August 1951 during which we established an official Atlantic record.

In 1952 we were involved in proving the full range capability of these aircraft, and finally planned flights across the Atlantic from Belfast to Newfoundland and back on the same day with official observation by the Royal Aero Club. This was a memorable event.

On the morning of 26 August 1952 under low overcast and in glistening rain, we started engines for what seemed to be just another routine Canberra test. Over the past three years these aircraft had flown so reliably that there no longer seemed to be an experimental or unknown element in these operations. You just signed the paperwork, climbed in and took off to do the scheduled job, and that was all there was to it except the sheer pleasure of every Canberra flight.

But now we were about to head off due west over 2000 miles of ocean and then come back the same way that day!

Our preparations had been conventional and professional and in identification of risk element we had established that for about 800 miles in mid-Atlantic in the event of one engine failure the only diversion options would be to Keflavik in Iceland or after that to Bluie West in Greenland. Both of these diversions would be problematic due to the likelihood of adverse weather, especially Bluie West which had to be approached at low level through a narrow, mountainous fjord and was often weathered out in any case.

There were no Atlantic rescue facilities at that period, and in any case a Canberra ditching would be impractical in stormy seas and the chances of survival after using ejection seats would be negligible.

In counterbalance the reliability of Canberras and the Avon engines over the past three years of intensive test flying had been exceptional, and so we had planned this as a normal test operation though with less than normal UK diversions for emergency.

Now, with Watson and Hillwood in the back and after dealing successfully with a temporarily off-line generator (*see* Appendix 8B), I obtained taxi clearance from Aldergrove Tower and moved out in the heavy rain towards the main runway.

In the reassuringly familiar cockpit I completed the pre take-off checks, ran up engines to full power against the brakes which did not slip at this heavy fuel weight, and with 'Clear Take-Off' from the Tower we began another confident and interesting day of Canberra testing.

Turning left in the rain immediately on becoming airborne and while the undercarriage was retracting, I held VX185 down below the 800ft cloud base in a full throttle 360 degree circuit back to overfly the Royal Aero Club observers by the main runway, and then at 450kt pulled smoothly up into cloud and on to the first compass heading called for by navigator Watson.

Settling into the climb at 400kt until intersecting Mach 0.7 with the Canberra nicely in trim under finger-tip control and adjusting engines to climb power, it was a pleasantly routine instrument reference flight until we broke out of the cloud tops at about 14,000ft with the sun rising directly behind and sending the sharp shadow of the Canberra skimming along the clouds below and ahead of us.

This was mainly an air-miles-per-gallon range – proving sortie and so the monitoring of fuel consumption and continuous management of the fuel system was already in progress.

At this point we loosened our ejector seat top-harness straps to provide comfort and ease of movement for the four hours ahead. We had agreed that emergency ejection over the Atlantic would not really be a viable option, but that sitting comfortably was! In any case, from our cruising altitude above 40,000ft there would probably be ample time to tighten the harness up again if needed.

After about fifteen minutes' climb we reached the planned initial cruise height of 41,000ft and I levelled, still at max. climb power until stabilising speed at Mach 0.74 which was to be held for the next four hours. Then, after trimming engines to max. continuous power, there was little else for me to do except continuously monitor engines and systems health and record at regular intervals the fuel state and progressive tank selections.

Each of the 2000 mile sectors of this operation (4,144 statute miles – Aldergrove to Gander and back) were flown manually there being no serviceable autopilot in VX185, and here the precision and ease of control typical of all Canberras was of prime importance.

Sitting back in the comfort and comparative quiet of this powerful but docile aeroplane there was no sense at all of the drama now building up back home in the UK press and radio about 'the double Atlantic flight'.

Hillwood, Watson and I were just engaged in another normal and very pleasant day of Canberra testing, but instead of routinely going round and round the skies of UK this one was going straight west – to America!

So it was in an atmosphere of relaxed calm but professional attentiveness that the crew of VX185 headed west over the endless cloud sheet.

Altitude increased steadily at constant Mach No. as the fuel burned off, and the first weather station was passed 500 miles west of Ireland at 44,000ft. A running fix from 'Ocean Station COKA's NDB (Non-directional beacon) had confirmed position and enabled Watson to calculate the effect and strength of the jetstream. It was on the nose at more than 100mph but calculation showed that, as planned, we had adequate fuel reserves to cover this.

And so the flight continued over the featureless cloud sheet with the sun rising only slowly behind us, not warming the cabin with solar radiation so that the navigator, Watson, began to feel the cold. Hillwood could move about so he came forward to the 'jump seat' by me where it was warmer!

After the next 500 miles a running fix was tried with 'Ocean Station Charlie', but with no result as they did not reply to our VHF calls. But eventually an R/T voice said he was a Canadian airliner bound for London and could he help. I said no thanks but it was nice talking to him. I gave our call-sign, 'Canberra 185', and he came back, 'Say, is that right that you are turning right round at Gander and going back to the UK?' So the news of this flight had spread. I replied, 'Affirmative,' and he said, 'Jees, what a helluva way to spend a day!'

This brought things into perspective as we cruise-climbed steadily on past 45,000ft with everything in perfect technical order, and the navigator working hard at his calculations in the absence of any further help from outside.

The probability of error over the last 1000-mile leg in the presence of known high-speed winds and the absence of any positive 'fixing' information was high, but Watson was confident and I knew as we pressed on to the west we were certain to reach the North American continent in due course!

After three hours of this entirely peaceful flight Watson made contact with St John's (Newfoundland) NDB and obtained a fine-angled 'running fix' that confirmed that we were comfortably close to the planned track, and then at an estimated 150 miles from the Newfoundland coast the cloud in the distance altered and gaps began to appear.

In the first large one a patch of bright blue water could be seen and on it a brilliant white spot – an iceberg, which was clear evidence that we were crossing the ice flow area running south from the Greenland/Baffin Land gap as we should be.

Presently Watson said, 'You should be able to see coastline any time. I think we are slightly north of track, steer port five degrees.'

I did so and then saw a shadow across the water in a cloud gap about fifty miles ahead, which as we neared it was clearly landfall.

'100 miles to run,' said Watson, 'start descending.' I confirmed that I would increase to Mach 0.8 in the descent and hold that until intersecting 485kt IAS.

Peter Hillwood was still on the jump seat and I asked if he wanted to go back and strap himself in, and he said, 'No, I'll help you identify the check point on Gander Lake'.

I confirmed this good idea and set the Canberra on its long, fast descent from 47,000ft at near Mach limits, which needed care with Hillwood not strapped in.

We descended through layered cloud over a rugged coastline and broke into the clear in the endless northern visibility over pine-forested, rocky hills with a myriad lakes and rivers, and then over to starboard white runways and buildings. Gander Airport!

Now in turbulence descending through 2000ft, a lake appeared dead ahead and, as I took 185 down over the water still at 485kt there was the white launch with RAeS observers.

Throttling back overhead at 500ft I turned starboard to bring Gander back into sight and called the Tower which responded, 'Canberra from Gander, you are clear to join left-hand circuit for main runway (giving heading). Number one to land. Call finals.'

Scarcely needing to touch the throttles I lowered undercarriage and flaps, retrimmed and flared this wonderful aeroplane gently onto Gander's long wide concrete strip, slowed and taxied back round the perimeter track to the Terminal. Flight time 4 hr 28 min and another routine test or another superb flight completed, whichever way you looked at it.

The specially-positioned Warton ground crew took over while I went to ATC for weather briefing and clearance for the return flight, enabling Hillwood and Watson to be driven off for a large steak second breakfast.

Our Canadian hosts seemed surprised when the crew said they would not have long enough to do justice to the hospitality. We had to explain that we were setting up a round-trip record and that we couldn't do that on the ground.

In forty-five minutes we were back at the now cleared and serviceable aircraft and after climbing aboard and just about to close the door, a jeep roared up and out came two lumber-jacketed figures carrying large bundles which they now thrust in through the hatch onto the cockpit floor – three very large smoked salmon, which certainly changed the atmosphere on the homeward flight!

I got on to the 'jump seat' beside Peter Hillwood who was to fly the return leg, and he now started engines and taxied out on this still fine and sunny morning (9 a.m. for them and midday for us).

With no other traffic we were cleared to go at once and after take-off Hillwood swept round in a wide right turn keeping low over the pine forest and accelerating to close to 500kt before bringing us down to 200ft over the observer's launch on the brilliant blue Gander Lake, then pulling up into a fast climb on track for our first easterly heading for Northern Ireland.

With only light strato-cu cloud at 5–6000ft Newfoundland's forests spread out in sparkling visibility ahead and to starboard, while over to port the rocky inlets and islands of the St Laurence gulf disappeared rapidly under our port wing.

Watson was still completing his navigation plan at this point and he said, 'With the expected wind we should have a flight time of 3 hr 20 min to Aldergrove.' One hour less than the outbound leg!

I had decided, on the evidence at the Gander Met. Office and our own plotting of the upper winds, that we would now forego the cruise-climb technique to fly a constant altitude taking full advantage of the jet-stream at our maximum practical cruise speed. So on passing 40,000ft and now back over full cloud cover in all directions, Hillwood levelled at 41,000ft and stabilised power to maintain Mach 0.77 initially. Then, after further deliberation with Watson about fuel consumption and margins, we increased the cruise to Mach 0.8 at which Hillwood was happy with unchanged controllability and with still a comfortable margin from the onset of compressibility buffet which we knew would appear beyond Mach 0.83.

Watson was busy with back-bearings on St Johns NDB and then as we came into VHF range of 'Ocean Station Charlie' he said, 'We've got over 100mph wind on our tail!' So we increased speed to Mach 0.81 for the last two hours.

In its usual serene way the Canberra was so quiet and undisturbed that it was difficult to believe that we were in fact storming across 2000 miles of ocean at over 600mph. There seemed remarkably little to do other than the navigation and systems monitoring and the regular fuel flow checks during the next 500 miles to the eastern weather station, 'Ocean Station COKA', which we passed to the north about two and a half hours after leaving Newfoundland.

'COKA' then passed Aldergrove's weather which was as we had left at 6.30 a.m., still cloud-base 800ft and poor visibility in rain but no further deterioration expected before a clearance from the west at around dusk.

This permitted our planned straight descent at high speed, and at an estimated 200 miles from the Irish coast and in VHF contact with Ulster radar we confirmed ETA and began a fast, shallow descent maintaining Mach 0.8.

Hillwood held this until intersecting 480kt IAS just below buffet onset.

Approaching the cloud tops at about 12,000ft Peter confirmed that he would hold this speed for cloud penetration as long as turbulence was not encountered.

And so we plunged into darkening cloud, the setting sun behind being already on the horizon, and with some bumps and a sudden increase in noise level as we ran into heavy rain which glared spasmodically round our wing-tip navigation lights, I wondered for a moment if we could rely on Watson to steer us to a safe cloud-break over Loch Neagh as we planned and not into the surrounding, unseen mountains!

But our approach and descent co-ordinated by Nutts Corner NDB and Aldergrove Radar, sounded secure and positive, so Hillwood pressed on down in the nil visibility gloom and harsh battering rain through 2000 to 1000ft on the altimeter at over 450kt IAS until dark shadows on either side and ahead broke into wispy views of rainswept fields and dykes below and a loch shoreline. Then out over leaden grey water with the shore stretching ahead on the starboard side.

'Loch Neagh,' said Watson with confidence, 'starboard on to 110 degrees. Aldergrove straight ahead.' There came the glistening runways with approach lights at full brilliance as Hillwood brought the Canberra down low over the drenched observers by the runway. The flight time from Gander Lake to Aldergrove had been 3 hr 26 min at an overall average speed of 605mph!

Power at idling, Hillwood took no time in turning finals and landing on the near-flooded runway and we taxied into the RAF base area where there was a large crowd including, we found, numbers of gentlemen of the press who apparently believed that the whole show was for them and that they were in charge.

After greetings by the RAF station commander who handed us a kind message from the Governor of Northern Ireland, we attended a brief Press call at which I gave a short account of the aims and results of the test, which some of the Press apparently regarded as out of order – this was a historic event and a PR exercise they said, and nothing to do with testing!

Then one said, 'Flying over all that ocean in one day must have been dramatic and stressful. Tell us about it.' I said, 'Afraid it wasn't and we shan't need any counselling!'

Saying our thanks to the RAF and to our Warton servicing team, we took off for Warton again in VX185; no refuelling had been necessary after crossing the

Back at Warton after the flight from Gander.

Atlantic at nearly full throttle all the way!

Over Douglas Isle of Man the skies were clear and the lights of Blackpool could already be seen as we began our final descent from 10,000ft.

Receiving clearance to land from the calm voices of the Warton controllers whom we had been talking to only twelve hours before with 4000 miles of ocean and a steak breakfast in Canada in between, VX185 landed smoothly at its Warton base in the dusk and taxied to its place on the north-west tarmac where a small group were waiting.

Jimmy Pickthall, the stalwart ground staff chief and his crew; Bob Hothersal, Warton Flight Shed Superintendent; and Freddy Page. And then a little apart our long-suffering wives.

No-one else from Works or design offices to welcome home 'their' aircraft – but then it was 6.30 p.m. and after knock-off time. We keep things in perspective in Lancashire!

As we walked across to the offices someone gave me a small brown envelope, and when we began to move off to explain our absences to our wives I opened the envelope – it was a telegram from Her Majesty the Queen.

The 'double Atlantic' was perhaps the most significant flight of the many records that were now being set by Canberras world-wide, both by my English

The author meeting Glen L. Martin, president of the Martin Co. in Baltimore during 1952.

Electric crews and by the skilled operators of the Royal Air Force.

Of two major operations by the latter in early 1951 the first was the tour of South America by a Bomber Command Canberra formation led by AVM Sir Dermot Boyle (later ACM Sir Dermot and after he retired, Chairman of British Aircraft Corporation).

This was an ambitious and very successful venture which resulted ultimately in Canberra purchases by four South American states, and it was not without some perilous moments!

The first stage included the first jet crossing of the South Atlantic, from Dacca to Recife, with in those days no navigation aids whatsoever over 1300 miles of ocean and none available at their destination!

Dermot Boyle described it as a strange experience to be poised at high altitude in mid-South Atlantic with no-one to speak to and absolutely no contact with the outside world! Eventually, when it was time to let down they entered high cloud and remained in it for what seemed a very long time until when still descending in rain and sleet they passed through 1000ft with absolutely nothing in sight! He began to wonder if they might miss their destination entirely! But, he said, there

The Bi8 development. Perhaps the finest of the Canberras, seen during its first flight during the summer of 1954.

had been no need to worry. His navigator John Brownlowe 'eventually hit South America right on the nose!'

Then, before the great RAF Canberra flights across the North Pole and the winning by the RAF against all comers in 1952 of the New Zealand Air Race, there had been the most significant Canberra event of all.

Before finalising their requirement for the acquisition of Canberras for the USAF, the 'Senior Officers Board' of the Pentagon had demanded in March 1952 to see a 'fly-off' competition between a Canberra and all the best competitors that could be put up by the great US aircraft industry, plus a CF100 from Canada.

The fly-off took place at Andrews Air Force Base, Washington (the home base of the Presidential aircraft 'Air Force One') and the Canberra won hands down.

It has since been said that the decision to purchase had already been taken and that the fly-off was political window-dressing; but there can be little doubt that if the Canberra had compared unfavourably with any one of its competitors that day any such decision would have been quickly overturned! There was a very powerful element in Washington that strongly opposed any idea of the USAF buying British!

But the procurement went ahead for over 400 B57 Canberras, and they proved to be the most successful night-attack aircraft for the USAF in the Vietnam war.

After the 'Argentine' demonstration May 1969. The 20th Anniversary. Left to right, Alan Watson, Jack Barlow, Bill Foxcroft and the author.

The Canberra has become, in fact, unique in aviation history. No other military jet aircraft has ever served for fifty continuous years and with more to come.

It has given immensely valuable service in a multitude of different roles and has been enjoyed by engineers for its quality, reliability and ease of maintenance, and by accountants for the same reason; it has always been a 'pilot's aeroplane'.

For me it was a privilege to be associated with the Canberra and subsequently with its Warton successor the Lightning for thirty of those fifty years, and with all the very special people who designed, built and tested these famous British aircraft.

They were the most enjoyable years of my flying life.

The Canberra's double Atlantic flight in 1952 caused great media interest, not least in the USA:

Morning Advertiser
27 August 1952
Britain's best air record
Canberra jet narrows Atlantic gap

A British Canberra jet bomber hurtled across the Atlantic and back yesterday in a record-smashing flying time of seven hours 59 minutes. The achievement which thrilled two hemispheres was completed between early-breakfast (6.36 a.m.) and tea-time (4.43 p.m.), with a two-hour stop at Gander, Newfoundland.

The Canberra's makers, English Electric Co, gave these unofficial timings for the two-way crossing (2,072.79 miles each way between starting and finishing lines): Outward: four hours 34 minutes, average speed 456 mph. Inward: three hours 25 minutes, average speed 606 mph (a West-to-East record). It was the first plane to make the double crossing in a day.

Daily Telegraph
28 August 1952
U.S. acclaims Canberra's feat
Tributes by press
From our own Correspondent New York Wednesday

New York newspapers today gave great prominence to news and pictures of the British Canberra jet bomber which yesterday broke all records for the two-way crossing of the Atlantic. An editorial in this afternoon's *New York Telegram-Sun* under the heading 'Whoosh!' said:

It was a stunt yes, but a useful one. It dramatises the age in which we live. It gives our own plane designers, builders and flyers something to shoot past, not just at. Our applause to the British and thanks for the competition.

In a leading article entitled 'The Shrinking World' the *New York Times* said:

This is a feat on which congratulations are due first of all to the valiant and skilful crew, and second to the British nation which, having lost the mythical Blue Riband of the Atlantic to the S.S. *United States*, has nailed a different and more modern riband to its mast.

It marks a new triumph for the British jet plane industry, which appears to be assuming the lead in the Western world in both military and commercial aircraft.

The newspaper added: 'It is a comfort it (the British aircraft industry) is on our side'.

Evening News
27 August 1952
Canberra flight a triumph, says U.S.
'Britain in the lead'

Tributes were paid today to the British Canberra's record-breaking transatlantic return flight.

The two-way crossing marks a new triumph for the British aircraft industry, said the *New York Times*.

The paper said: 'The British jet plane industry appears to be assuming the lead in the Western World in both military and commercial aircraft – and it is a comfort that it is on our side'.

'Heartening'

The *San Francisco Chronicle* said: 'The British have developed the Canberra to con-
found their enemies. We can be glad that so elusively fast and potentially destructive
an airplane is on our side and that in fact the production of American models of the
Canberra is to get under way'.

The *Melbourne Herald*, in an editorial headed 'Jet Triumph for Britain', said
Britain's two-year jet leadership over America included both civil and military aircraft and if such leadership brought the expected flow of orders from abroad the
industry would have the means of making still further progress.

'The prospect is heartening to a nation battling hard for trade and solvency. It is
equally cheering to Britain's allies'. – Reuter.

Daily Mail
28 August 1952
When the world shrank

*Most American newspapers put the Canberra's two-way Atlantic flight on yesterday's front page.
Some carried pictures and comments as well. Here are two of the comments.*

From the *New York Times*: 'Seismographs did not record it, but the world shrank
again yesterday when a British jet bomber established a new speed record and
flashed across the Atlantic and back again in ten hours of the same single day
and in exactly 7 hr 59 min actual flying time'.

The newspaper also said that this was a feat on which congratulations are due
'first of all to the valiant and skilful crew and second to the British nation which, having lost the mythical blue ribbon of the Atlantic to the S.S. *United States*, has nailed a
different and more modern ribbon to its mast.

'It marks a new triumph for the British jet-plane industry, which
appears to be assuming the lead in the Western world in both military and commercial aircraft – and it is a comfort that it is on our side'.

Church Times
29 August 1952
Mastery of the Air

Britain has now proved herself to be several years ahead of America in the development of jet-propelled aircraft. The British Comet is by far the fastest air liner on
regular service in the world. The Canberra jet bomber of the Royal Air Force has
this week added to its laurels by flying across the Atlantic and back in a mere eight
hours of one day. In the past week also the new Bristol Britannia passenger aircraft
has received its trials. The Americans are now so worried at the British lead in jet
aircraft, that General Eisenhower has found time, even in the middle of an election
campaign, to talk to United States experts in aircraft design on this subject. The
American designers want Government subsidies to help them catch up with their
British rivals.

The *Recorder*
30 August 1952
New air triumph
Why Canberra broke record

Three important needs led Britain and the English Electric Co to launch the magnificent Canberra jet bomber across the Atlantic in a spectacular quest of new Atlantic records on Tuesday.

Despite adverse weather conditions Wing Commander Beamont and his crew crossed the ocean both ways in the record total flying time of 7 hr 59 min. Thus they achieved brilliantly the objects of the flight. These were:

1. To discover more about an aeroplane whose actual powers and behaviour during long-distance high-speed are still largely theoretical.

Petrol consumption during adverse weather conditions, radio communications, navigation possibilities and the effect on the crew of such a flight – all these were carefully studied.

2. Both trade and political considerations are linked to such an outstanding achievement. Russia, for example, could not fail to be impressed, knowing that both the RAF and USAF are to be equipped with a plane with range and speed adequate for flying across its territory to a base in the Middle East.

3. All aircraft manufacturers wish to sell more planes. This flight will enable friendly foreign governments to choose from the contending makes more easily.

Flight
5 September 1952
Graceful tributes

American Press reaction to the Canberra's Atlantic records and, by implication, to Britain's jet progress in general, has been distinctly generous.

In spite of Presidential election news, the Canberra story found a place on many front pages. The *New York Times* congratulated the crew and the British Nation – 'which having lost the mythical blue ribbon of the Atlantic to the S.S. *United States*, has nailed a different and more modern ribbon to its mast. It marks a new triumph for the British jet-plane industry, which appears to be assuming the lead in the Western World in both military and commercial aircraft – and it is a comfort that it is on our side'.

This last thought was echoed in the *San Francisco Chronicle*: 'We can be glad that so elusively fast and potentially destructive an airplane is on our side and that in fact the production of American models of the Canberra is to get under way'.

Said the New York *World Telegram and Sun*: 'It was a stunt, yes, but a useful one. It dramatises the age in which we live. It gives our own plane designers, builders and flyers something to shoot past – not just at. Our applause to the British and thanks for the competition'.

New York's *Daily Mirror* commented candidly: 'Without meaning to sound sour-grapeish we would like to ask: "Where the hell is the United States?" Somewhere along the line, governmentally, militarily, commercially, we have let the British get way out ahead in jets. Pan-American World Airways is considering placing orders in Britain. This does not speak well for our illusion of American air power, either military or commercial. Anyway, congrats to the British'.

CHAPTER SIX

EXPORTING BRITISH AVIATION

Venezuela

Following the successful tour of South America in 1952 by the RAF's 101 Squadron Canberras led by Sir Dermot Boyle, a number of national air forces showed interest in equipping with the new and rapidly becoming famous jet bomber.

This was after the successful presentation of the Canberra to Pentagon officials at Andrews Air Force Base, Washington, by English Electric in 1951 which I had flown and which had resulted in the major contract for the USAF.

The exceptional performance and ease of handling of this small twin-jet bomber coupled with its demonstrated simplicity of maintenance and reliability had opened up world-wide interest, and the English Electric company was facing the need for rapid expansion to meet his demand.

This was all occurring in addition to our pressing programme to develop eight further versions of the Canberra for the RAF alone in parallel to the P1 programme for Britain's first genuine supersonic aircraft and its twice the speed of sound development, the Lightning.

The Warton design and flight test centre and the Preston and Samlesbury production factories were busy indeed and getting busier!

The first South American country to make a formal requirement for the Canberra was Venezuela, and in April 1953 I flew by airline out to Caracas to demonstrate a Canberra that had been delivered to them by the RAF since it was a 'Service' aircraft.

The delivery flight had been straightforward via Gander Newfoundland and Baltimore to Maracay, a VAF base north of the capital; and on 1 April I arrived there to demonstrate the Canberra to VAF officials. Then things began to deteriorate!

I walked out in the blazing equatorial sun to see the Canberra and talk to our servicing team in preparation for flying at about midday, but that didn't happen.

The VAF VIPs did not appear for a while by which time having unwisely been out on the tarmac waiting for them all the morning without a hat, I was very hot!

There was a further delay while the officials went to lunch and I, again unwisely, went for a beer with the company team at the nearby hotel.

By early afternoon I was told that all was ready but by then I had begun to feel distinctly unwell, apparently as a result of the sun, heat and beer! So here was a problem. Conventional practice and common sense clearly said 'no flying', but the circumstances seemed to demand no cancellation and as demonstrating the Canberra was normally an enjoyable experience and no problem at all, I confirmed that all was ready. I should have thought about that a little more!

Canberra aerobatics were indeed straightforward, but it was a bomber aircraft and the control forces were heavy in high speed manoeuvring – and there was no air-conditioning in that greenhouse of a perspex-covered cockpit!

All of this became very apparent when I taxied out under the still-blazing sun with a cockpit temperature which must have been well above 120°F. The next minutes of 'Canberra style' high 'G' turns well inside the airfield perimeter, rolling out into half-loops, aileron diving turns, low-level rolls and zoom climbs up to semi stall-turns, were completed in a flow of sweat which finally so flooded into my eyes as to make it dangerous to continue.

When I flowed down from the cockpit there was considerable and excited applause, but all I needed was a cold shower!

A bad night followed during which I vowed never to stand out in the tropics again without a hat, and then three things happened. Firstly the British Ambassador wanted to see me (the Embassy was fifty miles away at Caracas).

Secondly, the President of Venezuela wanted to see the Canberra perform on the morning of the following Monday at Caracas, and thirdly it was Friday and the weekend, which, we now learned, was to be a religious holiday and nothing would get done!

Our small team which consisted of the British Air Attache, W/Cdr Peter Hackforth (who had flown us in with his official Dove), the Rolls-Royce representative, the English Electric service engineer and, for no reason other than his voluntary offer, the resident de Havilland representative and myself repaired to the dingy hotel to make plans.

The Canberra would have to be serviced before flying up to La Calorta, the small grass airfield in Caracas. I would not be able to check the airfield with the Canberra first, but I had operated a Canberra off a rough grass airfield before near Paris so I accepted that. There was also a problem about starter cartridges.

The Ambassador, we agreed, would have to wait until after the President's display, and Peter Hackforth undertook to smooth the way for this!

Early next morning we were back at Maracay, but it was closed we were told firmly by the seriously armed guards at the gate! It took some time to overcome language difficulties and persuade the guard commander to let us in under escort as far as the hangar where, he said, the Canberra was.

The next problem was finding someone with a key to the hangar and when this was resolved the man said 'there are no personnel here and you won't be able to move your aircraft'. 'Oh yes we will,' we said and then came the next problem. The Canberra had been put at the back of the hangar with a VAF B25 Mitchell bomber in front of it – and on jacks!

It appeared that this had been done at the order of the senior USAF official 'advising' the VAF, before he departed for his weekend!

Things now began to add up. It had been expected that the USAF 'training mission' at Caracas would not be over-enthusiastic about an aggressive sales intrusion by the British, but we had not anticipated active obstruction and this was not to be the only example!

It was heavy work in the heat to get the Mitchell off its jacks and then push it outside, followed by the Canberra for engine checks – at this stage we had found that there was no tractor in sight, so we managed with manpower.

Then while the servicing work proceeded I walked down to the lake which bordered Maracay airfield. This was reed-fringed and teeming with wild life in the steamy heat including varieties of wading birds and some of the biggest insects I had ever seen, but suddenly out from the bank below me a large band-ed snake slid into the water and began swimming (or rather writhing) back in my direction. I did not like the look of him and retreated!

By late afternoon the Canberra was declared serviceable with one further problem. There were two engine starter cartridges left for each engine, and no spares nearer than the main sea-port some hundreds of miles away where, appar-ently, the cartridges and other vital supplies were held in bonded store and could not be reached until after the weekend!

It would need two (successful) cartridge starts to get the Canberra up to Caracas, and that would leave only one cartridge each to start the engines on the following Monday – and the cartridge starting system was not 100% reliable! Here was a dilemma. To call off the flight for the President on Monday, or take the risk and hope for the best.

With nothing to lose I took this course and prepared to fly to the capital on the next day (Sunday), but making a formal arrangement proved impossible. La Calorta aerodrome had no Air Traffic Controller on duty or any navigation aids, but the man on the telephone said he supposed it would be OK for us to come in, and that was it!

Peter Hackforth told me that 'there isn't any radio but Calorta is just over the mountains, just between the city of Caracas and a mountain to the north – you can't miss it'. 'What if there is cloud cover?' I said, and Peter replied, 'Never after midday – only in the early mornings!'

So with one of the engineers in the back seat I flew the Canberra up over the arid ridge of mountains towards the capital. With no radio or aids to navigation this was just a case of following a compass heading for a calculated time, hope-fully looking out for landmarks to identify on my rather indistinct map.

I had other things in mind as well. The grass aerodrome of La Calorta was quite short for a Canberra and the grass would need to be dry! So I now noticed with interest a build-up of cumulus cloud ahead which looked as if it might pre-cipitate on the mountains below!

But on time through a break in the now two-thirds cloud cover below I saw buildings spreading out ahead. It had to be Caracas and as I slid the Canberra carefully down through the cloud gap two things of interest emerged; the city dis-appeared ahead up another mountainside into cloud and there to my left was a circular parched brown airfield nestling between the northern edge of the city and the slopes of another steep mountain.

It looked very small as I circled, and presently a green light winked indicating I supposed that I was clear to land.

It looked quite dry and the only remaining question was how rough was the surface and would the Canberra's undercarriage cope? There was only one way to find out and so I lowered undercarriage and flaps and set up a low approach over the adjoining streets to touch down just inside the boundary.

After a lot of rumbling and thumping the Canberra slowed and I stopped engines near the one building which I assumed was the airport centre and ATC.

Presently a heavily armed guard emerged and initiated a stern conversation in Spanish which was still getting us nowhere when Peter Hackforth's Dove appeared and taxied in.

The combined efforts of our team finally persuaded the guard that even though I had no passport (it was in the hotel), he need not arrest me as I was not hostile and had come to meet the President, Perez Jimenez ('Perishing Menace' to the Brits of course!).

So far so good and after securing the Canberra for the night and reminding the guard that it was his responsibility to see that it was closely guarded for the President, we repaired to Peter Hackforth's villa in the city prior to visiting the Embassy.

The British Ambassador was highly amused by all these events but made it clear that the display on Monday must take place without a hitch. I thought again about our only two starter cartridges, but assured him that all would be well.

We then repaired to the villa of a lady described by the Hackforths as the doyen of the British expatriates in Caracas, where a party was in progress.

Our hostess did not seem much interested when Peter Hackforth introduced me as 'the pilot who is demonstrating the Canberra jet to the President tomorrow'.

But when he added 'and he recently flew a Canberra twice across the Atlantic – each way in one day,' she turned to me with a dazzling smile and said, 'What on earth did you do that for!'

I said, 'We wanted to see how much it would do to the gallon!' I didn't see much of her after that.

The following morning I awoke early, and looking out of my window to where the Caracas mountains should be there was only grey mist!

There were only two hours to go and at breakfast Peter Hackforth said 'it will burn off', but he did not say when!

At 7.45 a.m. the road to La Calorta was in thick mist and as we bumped across the grass towards the Canberra there was a light patch in the cloud above which gradually changed from grey to blue.

At eight o'clock there was enough blue above for the Canberra but the surrounding mountains were invisible, as was the far boundary of the aerodrome.

At 8.20 a.m. a cavalcade of cars appeared with heavily-armed motorcycle escorts, each flying the Venezuelan flag.

Meeting the President and the British Embassy staff I apologised for not having the language, and the President said it was unnecessary as his English was good!

I showed him the Canberra's cockpit, and talked a little about its remarkable performance.

The far boundary of the aerodrome was now just in sight and the blue patch overhead seemed about as big as the field – the Canberra could get round in this, but still the mist all round was solid with unseen mountains!

The President said that he would like the Canberra to fly, and I explained that without replacement starter cartridges I would not be able to land after the demonstration and would return to Maracay.

Signalling to the ground team I pressed the port engine starter – the cartridge fired and the engine revved up. Now for the final step, and the starboard engine lit with a comforting roar!

Now all we had to do was a tight demonstration virtually within the limits of the airfield, always remembering the close-by invisible mountain on the northern side, but this day was never going to be easy!

As the Canberra bumped and swayed over the rough grass towards the down-wind boundary and I concentrated on how best to make use of these restrictive conditions, the totally unexpected occurred in the shape of a DC-3/C-47 transport with wheels down approaching to land.

I waited until he had cleared the strip and in the absence of any radio or sig-nalled instructions I began to open up for take-off – but then another C-47 appeared out of the mist and another behind it!

This was clearly a troop movement, but after the third C-47 had landed I decided to go and with full power the Canberra leapt off into a tight left-hand turn climbing to establish the height of the cloud/mist base. This was about 800ft (above airfield level) and quite enough, so I pulled hard round and back down towards the small group of spectators and cars, levelled out over them and then entered a climbing roll during which I was impressed to see another C-47 approaching head-on with its wheels down!

There was actually no danger of a near-miss but I was now wondering how the President's 'command performance' of the Canberra had come to be prejudiced by a USAF-directed movement of VAF transport aircraft.

Completing a sharp 'wing-over' at the far boundary I brought the Canberra in a vertical bank round the airfield with, I suspected, spectacular condensation vor-tices streaming from the wing-tips in the humid air, and then bore back down for a full power run to about 450kt (about as fast as the conditions would permit), and then almost unbelievably another C-47 straight ahead with its wheels down but this time above my very low height!

Conventional air traffic rules were clearly not relevant and I held course to flash by under the C-47 whose pilot was probably more surprised at that stage than I was!

That seemed to be enough and the time to end this chaotic event, and so I pulled the Canberra hard round again and flew down the field towards the group who may have been by now spell-bound or livid with rage – I had no way of knowing.

With one final gesture for the benefit of anyone below who knew what was going on, in a high-G pull-up at full power I stood the Canberra on its tail, dis-appearing up into the mist and cloud on the direct heading for the Caracas mountain!

W/Cdr Peter Hackforth may have had near heart failure but I knew that I was soon in the vertical and that the unseen mountainside was not, and I hoped that we would clear the mist/cloud tops before I had to roll off the top to recover to level flight.

We cleared the tops into brilliant sunshine at about 5000ft over a white cloud sheet with no mountains in sight below, and then prepared for the next little problem. How to find Maracay if the cloud was solid there!

In the event, breaks began to appear below at ETA and there was the edge of the Maracay Lake.

It had been an interesting weekend and an unimaginable number of international air traffic regulations had been broken, so I wondered if there would be repercussions.

In discussion with the Embassy staff I took the view that whoever had authorised the C-47 transport movement in total disregard of the President's instruction for a Canberra demonstration was probably now in trouble, and that my transgressions of AT rules might not be commented on, especially as the Canberra's flying for the President was by now all over the Caracas papers!

The Ambassador agreed with this, but added a rider that it might be a good idea if I took the first plane home which I did the next day! There were no reverberations from this event other than praise for the Canberra which went on to serve the VAF well for over twenty years.

New Zealand

The decade of the 1950s was a busy time for English Electric, and with an immensely saleable product in their Canberra jet bomber the company's sales and service departments, led firstly by Strang Graham of the London office and latterly by Glen Hobday from Warton, were successful in establishing the Canberra in fifteen air forces world-wide.

In parallel, the development at Warton of the English Electric P1 supersonic technology demonstrator into the Lightning all-weather fighter with twice the speed of sound capability had, by 1958, become a brilliant success but, as with so many other projects of great potential in the period, all government support had been withdrawn from the programme in the 1960s just at the point when it was needed to capitalise on the brilliance of its design and to develop its full potential for the export market.

'There is no chance of exporting the Lightning,' was a statement from English Electric's own London office in 1962, who were by then totally demoralised by the government policy to 'finish with the Lightning as soon as possible'.

At Warton there was a different view. After eight years of continuous personal experience with this exceptional aircraft, and of close contact with the pilots of Fighter Command who were unanimous in their high praise of the Lightning which had more than doubled their performance in the quantum step forward from their previous Hunters (although the engineering branch were less enthusiastic), I had strongly advised the company to undertake private-venture development to improve the range, armament and role capabilities of the Lightning specifically to challenge the American bid in 1965 for a contract with vast potential to set up an entirely new supersonic defence system for Saudi Arabia.

A BAC Strikemaster on test for the RNZAF. With L-R tanks and Matra rocket launchers.

The company took the courageous decision in 1965 and our bid was successful, and so began in 1966 the British export programmes 'Magic Carpet' and 'Magic Palm' which led to the famous 'Al Yamamah' contract which has, in renewals over three decades with more to come, three times been officially recorded as 'Britain's biggest-ever and most valuable export programme'.

There were of course other sales ventures which were less successful, such as attempts in Australia with the TSR2 (1963) and Tornado (1974).

Both of the latter met with cool receptions and the clear message from RAAF headquarters, Canberra that they could make better use of their time than listening to presentations on 'inferior British equipment by whingeing Poms'. They did, of course, buy American and suffered severe cost over-runs subsequently (to three times original estimates), and also long delays to full operational effectiveness, with both the F111 and the F18.

The Strikemaster was more successful and when in 1966 it had become apparent that the New Zealand air force needed a jet trainer (they already had our Canberra bombers), in the absence of the sales manager who was on a mission elsewhere I was charged by Freddy Page with leading a team consisting of a financial man, a service engineer and a member of the sales staff.

There was some urgency as we learnt that negotiations were already in progress in New Zealand with the Italian company Macchi for their jet trainer which had already been purchased, rather unwisely we thought, by the Australians.

After a hurried weekend of preparation we set off across the Atlantic, Canada and the Pacific to New Zealand, only after a wordy argument with our financial director who insisted that the way to New Zealand was via India and Singapore – 'everyone knew that'!

BOAC's VC10 airliners were the finest of all to travel in at that time, and Peter Grocock and I settled comfortably into the superb first class with the less senior members of our team in the back end – a 'politically incorrect' arrangement but I doubt if that thought occurred at the time!

Arriving the next day at Auckland we transferred immediately to a Fokker Friendship for Wellington, and arrived in mid-afternoon in a raging storm which was causing crosswinds on the airport's short runway, approaching the maximum strength before landings became impossible.

Struggling through the gale to the airport buildings we were told that this was nothing unusual and that the city was not called Windy Wellington for nothing!

We checked into our hotel which seemed almost as windy inside as the outside – the carpets on the floors were literally airborne – and with jet lag beginning to take effect we ordered a pot of tea over which there was some difficulty – it was apparently 'after tea time' – and we prepared to make plans.

Then the bombshell! The day's papers in the residents' lounge had banner headlines, 'Air Force to have new jet trainer. Defence Minister flies in Macchi jet', with pictures of Robert Muldoon (who later became Prime Minister) in the cockpit.

It seemed that fast action was needed, but first we would see the six o'clock TV news to update our scanty knowledge of what was actually going on.

At about 5.50 p.m. we sat around the TV set in the lounge with our cups of tea – and when we woke up it was 6.30 p.m. and the news was over!

Though desperately tired there was no going to bed until firm arrangements could be made and with the agreement of the team I told our agent, who had by then turned up, that I wanted an interview on national TV next morning essentially before we had any meetings with Air Force or government officials.

We had gauged this correctly and I was closeted with the TV presenter early next morning. I was glad to find that the interview was to be recorded and not live as it soon began to take an unsuitable line – 'Why have you people come over here when the government has already decided on the Macchi?'

I discontinued at this point and said that I would not take part unless the presenter was not only impartial but would put a specific question to me – 'Why do you think the government are favouring the Macchi option?'

They accepted these terms and in the interview I replied, 'Well, it couldn't have been for reasons of technical merit!'

This was put out almost immediately, and when back at our hotel making plans for visits to Airforce headquarters and possibly the airbase at Ohakea I was summoned for an urgent call from the Defence Ministry – the Minister wanted to see me immediately!

When I was ushered into his office Muldoon did not rise but said, 'You should not have said that on TV!'

I said politely that as the media were apparently under the impression that the Italian trainer was technically superior to the British contender and that this was, we believed, inaccurate, we were entitled to make this point.

'Nevertheless,' Muldoon said, 'you shouldn't have made it on TV!' It was quite clear that having made a strong political statement in arranging for the Australians to send one of their Macchis to Wellington and to fly him in it in full planned view of the media, my intervention was now seen as embarrassing.

But he did not pursue the point and asked a number of well-informed questions about the Strikemaster before saying, 'Well, the Air Force will want to hear all you've got to say tomorrow!'

I mentioned some of the commercial and after-sales advantages that the company would offer in a contract, and he said, 'Thank you very much,' with I thought only thinly veiled sarcasm. We clearly had an obstacle to surmount in the New Zealand Minister of Defence!

But next day at the Air Headquarters we were received well and subjected to balanced and professional questioning, during and after which I gained the feeling that the New Zealanders had noted with some surprise that some of the operational defects that they had detected in the Macchi aircraft were not present in our Strikemaster.

Finally, we were told that our presentation had been appreciated and that the 'competition was not over'!

That night we had dinner with one of the staff of the British High Commission during the course of which it became very apparent that he did not understand or had not been briefed effectively on why we were there.

He seemed highly excited about the TV interview and said it should never have happened, but by then we were suffering mild hysterics at this bizarre situation.

Here, at the end of our difficult and high pressure negotiation was a British official telling us that we were out of order and only causing embarrassment to no good purpose!

In the lift going down, and largely I suppose as a result of jet lag and the tensions of the past two days, hilarity took over and we were suddenly overcome with compulsive and uncontrollable laughter. We staggered into our hotel still with tears in our eyes, and the next day set off back across the Pacific for home.

Back at Warton jet-lagged again, Freddy Page (whom we had kept informed by cable) was rather concerned about the tone of the negotiations, and then I came under fire from an unexpected quarter. The sales manager, who had been occupied elsewhere, launched an attack on our conduct of the mission saying it was quite inappropriate to 'go on TV'.

I think there was an element of pique in this, but we heard no more from the critics after the RNZAF confirmed (within a few days) their intention of purchasing Strikemasters!

CHAPTER SEVEN

'COMPRESSIBILITY' – THE SOUND BARRIER

The Transonic 1940s and the Supersonic 1950s

More than fifty years have passed since the speed of sound was exceeded in level flight by the Bell XS1 research aircraft flown by Major Chuck Yeager of the USAF, and since then much has been said and written on the subject of 'the Sound Barrier' and how it was overcome by the pioneer scientists, engineers and test pilots.

It was indeed a time of folklore with pilots probing into areas of high risk to prove or disprove the theories of scientists who could not share the risks.

Yet in the 1990s revisionist writings and TV programmes continued to add confusion to the history of what was, in fact, a straightforward though difficult and dangerous period of research.

Contrary to the popular belief promoted over the years by the ever-enthusiastic media, and periodically by aviation authors who either failed to research the subject thoroughly or used selective evidence to build a slanted view, the era of supersonic research in this country did not arrive with the headline catching 'Sonic Bangs' of the emergent swept-wing fighter prototypes at the Farnborough displays of the late 1940s, but it began at Hawker's Langley factory and test centre much earlier in 1942.

By 1950 practical knowledge established the hard way by trial and error at the factories and test establishments during the previous decade, had begun to come to fruition with new experimental aircraft which could by then dive to the speed of sound without the loss of control that had resulted when all the last generation of propeller-driven fighters had been dived to their limits at altitude.

This loss of control had occurred at speeds between seventy per cent and eighty-five per cent of the speed of sound varying with the types and, during the five years of World War II, continuous research and test flying had at last eliminated the mystery and established both understanding of the causes of the phenomenon and the means of making progress through what had begun to be thought of as a finite barrier to further increase in aircraft performance.

The problem had first emerged in the fierce air fighting of the early 1940s when fighter pilots of both sides had begun reporting control difficulties when diving at high speeds in combat at high altitudes, and there were some reports of fighters which had not suffered combat damage diving into the ground.

By 1941 the test establishment in Germany, Rechlin the *Reichsluftfahrt-ministerium* test centre, had become actively involved in investigations of this phenomenon, followed progressively by the manufacturers, Hawker and Supermarine in this country, Messerschmitt and Focke Wulf in Germany, and in

America most of the fighter manufacturers and the USAF test centre at Wright Field. RAE Farnborough's Aero Flight became involved from 1943 onwards.

The initial research had been inconclusive, but from 1942 onwards a new generation of more powerful and faster fighter prototypes appeared and they all without exception experienced a clear new limitation – at high altitude they encountered varying degrees of loss of control before they could reach their structural design limit dive speed (V_{ne}).

The fighters concerned were at Hawker the Typhoon; at Supermarine the later series Spitfires; in Germany the Bf 109G and FW 190 variants, and from 1943 onwards the Me 262 jet and the Me 163 rocket fighters; and in USA the Republic P47 Thunderbolt, the Lockheed P38 Lightning, the Vought Corsair and the North American P51 Mustang.

At Hawker the pilots involved from 1942 in this new and hazardous research flying were chief test pilot George Bulman, Philip Lucas, Ken Seth Smith, Bill Humble and in 1943, the author; and at RAE Farnborough Aero Flight test pilots one of whom, Tony Martindale, eventually dived a Spitfire to Mach 0.9 losing his propeller and reduction gear in the process and still managing to land safely.

In Germany as early as 1941 Heinrich Beauvais at Rechlin had investigated the loss on test of a Bf 109 in a vertical dive by repeating the dive conditions in hazardous circumstances, and also later in FW 190s; and in 1943 Mano Zeigler encountered similar difficulties but at higher speeds in the new Me 262 jet (which became in 1944 the world's first operational jet fighter).

In America in 1943 Col Cass S. Hough led the US test pilots in the investigation of loss of control at high diving speeds that began to be experienced in P47s and P38s, and in late 1944 Major Fred Borsordi, a USAF test pilot at the Wright Field test centre, brought back for the first time photographs of shock-waves blooming above the wing of a P51 at around Mach 0.85.

In 1943 I was attached to Hawkers at Langley from the RAF, replacing experimental test pilot Ken Seth Smith who had been killed in a Typhoon dive test, and I immediately became closely involved with the research (by then well advanced) into 'compressibility'. This was the term coined to describe the aerodynamic phenomenon that, it had now been discovered, caused this disturbing and limiting loss of control in combat conditions.

When a conventional straight-wing aircraft approaches the speed of sound the air ahead of it compresses in waves until, at 80% or more of that speed (Mach 0.8), the waves are condensed to a virtual wall or barrier approaching Mach 1 where the air will compress no more. Locally around the airframe, airflow accelerated to the speed of sound results in these waves breaking up into 'shock waves' which move erratically over wing, tail and control surfaces, causing variations in trim and control forces (hinge moments) and changes to the centre of pressure and resulting in severe reductions in stability and controllability.

These changes led to heavy buffeting, vibration, pitch trim changes and wing dropping with variations according to the type of aircraft. Together with an also characteristic severe drag-rise, they created an impenetrable barrier to increasing speed in the dive and eventually led to actual loss of control as the aircraft rolled

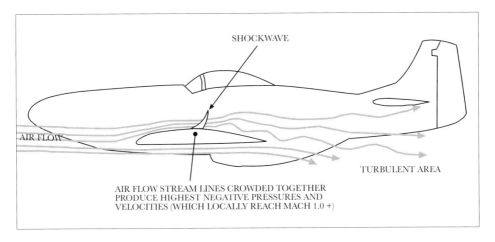

The typical pattern of airflow in 'compressibility' relative to a P51 Mustang, straight-wing fighter.

uncontrollably and pitched down against the pilot's maximum restraining efforts with the controls.

All this was accompanied by a roaring noise-level and violent buffeting; for the pilot a frightening experience for the first time and always an impressive one thereafter!

There were a number of cases of fatalities during this worrying period in the 1940s, but testing experience coupled with the increasing understanding of the scientists began to indicate that this loss of control could be linked to critical Mach No. (the relationship of the speed of the aircraft to the speed of sound) and not specifically to indicated airspeed. Testing also indicated that if when in an uncontrollable compressibility dive the test pilot 'rode it down' to lower altitude, the shock-waves would subside as the Mach No. became progressively lower in the denser air and control effectiveness would return slowly enabling recovery to level flight at 10,000ft or lower.

It was an encouraging theory and was proved by systematic dive testing; but it always remained an interesting experience to enter a full throttle dive in a Typhoon or later a Meteor, Vampire or Canberra, knowing that if you ignored the compressibility buffet threshold and did not pull out before reaching 'Mach Crit.' then you were in for an uncontrollable dive down to low altitude!

This practical knowledge amassed in the war years enabled the aero-dynamicists and designers to make progress towards resolving the problem. The first series of experimental prototypes in the late 1940s with wing-leading edges swept back for this purpose were shown to have improved controllability up to around 90 per cent of the speed of sound, but with relatively thick wings they were still severely limited by deteriorating controllability, drag-rise and compressibility roughness above this. However some, such as the Sabre, Swift and Hunter prototypes, were able to reach and slightly exceed Mach 1 in steep dives, although still with much reduced controllability at that point.

Before these began their trials in the late 1940s chief test pilot Geoffrey de

The Hawker P1 081 transonic research fighter. Chief Test Pilot 'Wimpey' Wade was killed in this during 1948.

Havilland had been killed in a compressibility dive in the DH108 tailless research aircraft, as had Hawker Chief Test Pilot 'Wimpey' Wade in the Hawker research aircraft for the Hunter programme – the P1081 with swept wings and tailplane.

In Germany early official research into the possibilities of supersonic flight had begun in 1940 at the state research institute DFS, and in the period 1941–43 this organisation produced a number of high-speed research prototypes with differing configurations and power sources, which led to the ultimate development, the DFS 346.

This high-fineness-ratio swept-wing design commenced construction at the Seibel factory in 1944 with a forty-five degree swept-wing of symmetrical section, a 12 per cent thickness-chord ratio and a high 'T' tail; and it was to be powered with two tail-mounted liquid fuel HWK 109-509 B-1 rocket engines.

This ambitious design was aimed at ultimately achieving Mach 2 (twice the speed of sound), but with the rapid German collapse in 1945 against the Allied forces this very advanced prototype never flew in Germany, and much of the design and development programme was captured by the Soviets in 1945 and transported from the Seibel plant to the Russian Central Aerohydrodynamic Institute. There, now named Samolyot 346, it became the basis for an active Russian research and development programme that eventually achieved supersonic level flight.

The author flew the second prototype Sabre, PU 598, to Mach 1 plus at Muroc in June 1948, having been briefed by North American Chief Test Pilot, George Welsh (seen flying the first prototype in this picture).

According to the aviation historian Henry Mathews, this occurred on 14 September 1951 flown by ex-Seibel test pilot Ziese, and the aircraft reached 1350kph (839mph) before becoming uncontrollable and breaking up. Ziese catapulted out in the nose-cone escape system and landed by parachute, breaking his leg (source Henry Mathews, Beirut air historian).

Russia had achieved supersonic level speed with this basically German design, but America was already there with the 'X' series of supersonic research aircraft and Britain and France were to follow shortly.

All these early experiences up to the late 1940s including French and American research, had led to confident belief that the adverse effects of compressibility could be reduced and possibly eliminated by a new approach to supersonic aerodynamics involving much thinner aerofoils and/or high wing-sweep angles. In America, in a courageous development and testing programme, the final breakthrough was achieved in 1947 when Chuck Yeager flew the

The roll-out of English Electric P1 in August 1954 at Boscombe Down.

rocket-powered thin/straight-winged Bell XS1 to a level Mach 1.06 over the Mojave Desert, while at the same period George Welsh was diving the North American XP86 Sabre swept-wing fighter prototype in controlled flight at Mach 1.

In this country we had lost the race due solely to gross government incompetence and interference in 1947 with the arbitrary cancellation of the Miles M52 supersonic research aircraft, and the British aviation industry had had to continue with hazardous dive testing by de Havilland, Hawker and Supermarine test pilots on developments in the DH108, Hunter and Swift programmes into the early 1950s. But none of these projects was ever going to result in a true supersonic fighter.

However, following pressure by W. E. W. Petter's English Electric design team in 1948 a Ministry contract was placed in 1949 on the Preston-based company for the F23/49, a research aircraft with potential for development into a fully supersonic fighter. This was the English Electric P1.

So, by the summer of 1954, having had by then personal experience of

The P1's first photographic session in September 1954. Precision control in evidence already.

seventy-two experimental dives to partial or in some cases complete loss of control in compressibility in Typhoons and Tempests, Meteor IVs and Canberras, together with many partially controlled transonic dives in Hunters and P86s, it was with a comfortable feeling of having been there before that I prepared to fly the third flight of the English Electric P1, WG760 at Boscombe Down on 11 August 1954. My first two flights with the P1 had been very successful and English Electric were now poised to investigate the unknowns of behaviour in this radical new sixty-degree swept-wing prototype in high Mach flight.

English Electric's brilliant young team of innovative engineers responsible for the hugely successful Canberra, were confident that in the P1 they would have the first British breakthrough to practical supersonics, but now it had to be tested!

After its steep three minute climb to 30,000ft the P1 was soon hurtling up-Channel in clear sunny weather past Selsey Bill in smooth, vibration-less level flight under perfect finger-tip control at over Mach 1, and with no compressibility effects apparent at all!

P1 WG760 on its first landing at the 1955 Farnborough Air Display.

WG760 was eventually tested to Mach 1.53 in 1966 and shortly after this Peter Twiss in the Fairey FD2 extended the official world airspeed record over a two-way measured course to beyond 1100mph. This speed was exceeded during the testing of the English Electric P1B (XA847, developed from the P1), which I first-flighted in May 1957 from Warton and then reached the initial RAF requirement at Mach 1.7 within two months in this brilliant fighter.

A year later, with the majority of this prototype's very successful programme completed I was again privileged to fly some of the new American 'century series' supersonic fighters for comparison with our Lightning, and during this visit to the Californian Mojave Desert I reached Mach 2, twice the speed of sound, in an early production Lockheed F104 from Palmdale.

The F104 was indeed impressively fast, but at that stage of its development it was not pleasant to fly and seemed very unlikely to realise its original intention as an air superiority fighter. It was no match at all for our Lightning in operational flexibility.

By contrast the XF106 (second prototype) which I flew next at the Edwards Flight Test Centre and which was still in early development, seemed likely to have similar performance to the Lightning though with less manoeuvrability at

Second P1 at Warton, 1955, with ventral tanks and guns.

First Flight of P1B/Lightning from Warton in May 1957, flown by the author.

VIP – Prince Bernhardt with the author and the P1 in 1954.

altitude, and to have a potentially superior weapons system.

Returning to Warton with this confirmation that the great American industry was no longer ahead of Britain in this field, with the Warton team I returned to the final stages of exploration of the Lightning's capability; and after progressive and successful tests beyond Mach 1.8 from early November, finally on 12 December 1958 I reached Mach 2.0 in smooth, vibrationless, stable and precisely controllable flight – the first British aircraft at twice the speed of sound.

At this tremendous speed there were still vital tests to be done. With these completed I began the deceleration turn in a wide sweep from Dumfries, across the Solway until heading south over Windermere for Warton still above Mach 1 until finally subsonic again descending over Morecambe Bay. (*See* Appendices 9 and 10.)

It was all so smooth and uneventful as to seem almost an anticlimax after all these years of struggling with 'into-and-out-of compressibility' dives.

But there was a sense of satisfaction. Now we had a real, capable Mach 2 fighter – and it was British.

"Had a little trouble losing cockpit canopies, but I think we've mastered it."

Reproduced from PUNCH, May 9 1956

The P1 lost three canopies during the early trials, all at supersonic speeds. The US magazine Aviation Week *said 'one canopy you can lose, two is unlikely but three - never!' The figure in front of the 'Whitehall Warriors' is Lord Nelson of English Electric. Cartoon by Chris Wren.*

Britain had recovered its lost years since the cancellation of the Miles M52 in 1947. The 'Sound Barrier' was a myth of the past and the way ahead was clear to the practical supersonic aircraft of the future such as the TSR2, Jaguar, Concorde, Tornado and Eurofighter 2000 Typhoon.

Supersonic over England

In more ways than one 1954 had been a new threshold in British aviation. Since 1940 fighter designers and research establishments in this country, Germany and the USA had been wrestling with the new problems of stability and control being encountered at high subsonic speeds, and for many years transonic and supersonic flight seemed beyond reach.

The breakthrough had come in USA when from 1947 the 'X' series of rocket-powered research aircraft were successful in making very brief level runs at and beyond the speed of sound.

In this country following the faulted government decision in 1947 to cancel its own promising supersonic research aircraft, the Miles M52, hazardous research testing was continued with the DH108 and developments of the Hawker and Supermarine swept-wing fighters leading to the Hunters and Swifts of the early 1950s.

These first swept-wing types could reach speeds approaching supersonic, but only in partial control and in nearly vertical dives lasting only seconds.

Then when the English Electric P1 technology demonstrator for the future Lightning supersonic fighter was being prepared for its first flight, the question arose: where to test it in continuous supersonic flight?

American experience had already confirmed that the shock-wave from an aircraft going through Mach 1 in level flight caused a continuous double-boom along its flight path on the ground below.

This was expected to be unacceptable to the populations of affected areas, so at the planning stage English Electric proposed a short supersonic range over a very low population area in the Pennines from north of Preston to Appleby, which was conveniently close to the P1's base at Warton.

The Ministry of Supply turned this down at once saying that supersonic tests

The P1B, Lightning prototype XA847 at Warton in 1957.

must be carried out over the sea, but when we pointed out that an earlier MOS regulation which was still in existence, expressly forbade testing prototypes over the sea due to risk of loss of evidence in event of a crash, they said that it would all have to be reconsidered!

So that in the event P1 testing at supersonic speeds did begin over the Pennine route in November 1954, and it eventually reached Mach 1.5 at which point the energy overpressure in the turn back towards base caused such consternation in the Appleby area that their MP raised a question in Parliament; and that facility was withdrawn forthwith!

The P1 was put back on the Irish Sea run from Great Orme Head to south of Dumfriesshire, which became an effective route for Warton's intensive Lightning, Jaguar and Tornado supersonic test programmes for the next twenty-five years. But there were further problems at first.

The spread of the supersonic boom was proved to vary from fifteen to twenty miles each side of track and this could just be fitted in safely by accurate navigation midway between Douglas, Isle of Man, and the Westmorland coast in the area from Barrow to St Bees Head; but only in still-air conditions.

We soon found that wind-shear could displace the boom pattern and that a strong easterly wind could result in booming the Isle of Man, and a westerly would affect Westmorland.

It was not long before questions were raised in Parliament on behalf of the Isle of Man whose citizens were understandably not appreciating these strange

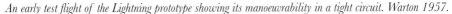

An early test flight of the Lightning prototype showing its manoeuvrability in a tight circuit. Warton 1957.

The Lightning development aircraft 725 with Red Top missiles and extended ventral tank taken at Warton circa 1960, with the author in the cockpit.

explosions that were now disturbing the tranquillity of that lovely island!

MOS wrote to my chief, Freddy Page, demanding our proposals for dealing urgently with the problem.

I believed, based on past experience, that 'openness' and a clear explanation of how and why this situation had occurred would most probably be successful, expecting that the Ministry authority would carry out this obvious exercise with the Isle of Man authorities themselves.

Not so. The Ministry merely told the House of Keys that 'the company responsible' namely English Electric, would come to Douglas to make a presentation, with their agreement of course.

In due course a sternly worded invitation was received for our representatives to report to the House of Keys, giving the date and timing, and Freddy Page told

The author taxying out at Palmdale in 1958 in a production Lockheed F104 Starfighter - 'a rather nasty little aeroplane but it could get to Mach 2'.

me to make the appropriate arrangements.

This needed precise handling and I decided that a large delegation with all relevant specialists would not be appropriate.

So, with the valuable assistance of Jimmy Dell we prepared an illustrated and professional presentation covering all the technical, regulation and public-relations aspects that constricted our operations in this vital test programme.

Dell and I flew to lovely Douglas in our communications 'Dove', and we were met and driven to the House of Keys by a senior executive.

In the old building we were shown directly into a splendid panelled hall redolent of the island's history and tradition and found, not a small group of executives but quite a large gathering of representatives of the House.

Introductions were polite but, I thought, quite stern and cool. There was no doubt that we were considered to be the cause of unjustified disturbance to their population – why could the disturbance not be shifted to those they considered responsible, the population and government on the mainland!

I had been briefed to expect something on these lines of course, but it was now clearly up to us.

I began by describing the need to test Britain's next generation fighter for the

Sir Thomas Pike of Fighter Command flies the T4 prototype with the author at Warton.

defence of this country in the role that had been demonstrated so convincingly in the Battle of Britain. And as to the necessity for this in this nominally peaceful age, who could claim convincingly that there would never be another threat to this country's airspace?

Beyond that who could claim that our ground and coastal sea forces would no longer need air protection?

The RAF needed supersonic interception capability now, and the English Electric Lightning would provide that superbly; and I described the pattern and extent of the supersonic boom path.

Jimmy Dell then made a concise, professional presentation on how we conducted the trials within the severe limitations imposed by the regulations

'Young Nelson', George Nelson Jr, with Sir Harry Broadhurst and Sir Thomas Pike at Farnborough as the author prepares to demonstrate the Lightning (with no restrictive SBAC rules!)

and by our own PR-related caution.

The senior executive thanked us for our 'clear presentation' and then said, 'Now is the time for lunch!'

On the way to the hotel and during a splendid meal the atmosphere changed remarkably. We were told that our visit had cleared the air, explaining many things that had not been appreciated; and in a general atmosphere of relief we were told that there would be no more complaints if we could keep incidents down to a minimum; that IOM would support 'this important UK programme' and would feel that in doing so they would be contributing to it – which indeed they did.

On returning to Warton, Freddy Page listened to our report with his usual lack of immediate enthusiasm – probably quite rightly!

But very soon a letter from the Minister of Defence to our Chairman, Lord Nelson, thanked the company for the measures taken at the House of Keys, and

A Lightning development aircraft with the prototype 'Mk 3' fin. Warton 1960.

concluded, '. . . Beamont and Dell had a great success in Man'!

It was another of many examples through the years of the importance and effectiveness of direct discussion with the people likely to be affected in the event of disturbances of any sort caused by aircraft noise. Tell people what it is about and why and they will generally end up supporting the effort if it is a justifiable cause.

And so Warton's 'Test Run Alpha' continued to be a valuable facility for the next twenty-five years, enabling the massive Lightning test programme to be completed unhindered during which the first British aircraft (Lightning) reached Mach 2.0 (twice the speed of sound) and beyond; and then the TSR2, Britain's first supersonic bomber, was taken to Mach 1.1. This was followed by all the British Jaguar supersonic test programme and lastly the great Tornado development programme.

These all continued on 'Alpha' with no complications and very few minor incident complaints until, one day in 1979, a Warton test pilot left his brains in the

The author landing the prototype Lightning XA847 on the first day of Farnborough in 1957.

briefing room, went out for his next Tornado test and ended it barrelling down 'Test Run Alpha' in the wrong direction at supersonic speed, straight towards Liverpool Bay!

He boomed a large part of South Lancashire including St Annes, Preston, Stockport, Liverpool and Southport, and 'Test Run Alpha' was withdrawn by the Ministry the next day!

All subsequent supersonic testing of Tornados and the Warton EAP technology demonstrator for the NATO Eurofighter/Typhoon, had to be carried out on a less favourable route across the Irish Sea (to stop well short of Dublin) until 1999 when after twenty years, Derek Reeh, the Warton director of Flight Operations (my third generation successor) and lead test pilot for the Eurofighter, obtained reinstatement of 'Test Run Alpha' for this vitally important test programme on the basis that his team of disciplined and highly professional experimental test pilots would, without difficulty, ensure the operation of 'Alpha' safely and in the right direction!

Over all the years since 1954 overland supersonic flight has been quite rightly banned, and the great Concorde test programme had to be conducted over sea routes around the British Isles and over the Bay of Biscay for this reason.

All RAF and NATO exercises around the UK have been similarly limited to supersonic sea routes. Maybe in time technology will develop means to suppress or eliminate the 'overpressure' disturbances from supersonic flight, but this is not yet in sight.

It has been a long sixty years of probing and evaluation, but now at least we know that the supersonic booms can never be tolerated overland and while

The author piloting a production Lightning 6 over the Pennines in 1964.

military aircraft in war situations may well continue to be used in this way, the future for a supersonic replacement for Concorde seems very uncertain.

Concorde has only been permitted to operate supersonically over water and this has been the basic reason for its failure to sell to airlines committed to overland routes.

In retrospect, the early problems with test routes for our P1 were a valuable stepping stone in the advance to the limited world of supersonic aviation.

Experimental Test Flying

In general, the activity under this heading continues progressively without drama as it has been preceded by intensive fault and risk analysis at every stage in the design, and in the current fashionable way by 'virtual reality' simulation programmes that aim to reveal problem areas before committal of the prototype to flight.

At the test-flying stage therefore, the task is now said to be to 'prove the validity of the simulation', and not the correct functioning of the aircraft, 'which has already been established in the simulator'.

Yet prototype aircraft still encounter technical troubles in flight test, recent examples being the Swedish Gripen and the American YF22, and all human endeavour carries the potential of human error which can occur in computer programming just as it can in systems engineering design or any of the other essential disciplines. Events involving risk to crews or hazard to the aeroplane are less frequent than in the past, but when they do occur they can focus attention!

One such incident occurred during the initial flights of the BAC TSR2, for its time a very advanced supersonic aircraft, specified for operational service in the RAF for thirty years or more from the early 1970s.

Due largely to an overcomplicated procurement and management system this aircraft had overrun its build target dates significantly, and when it commenced trials it still carried serious problems in engines, undercarriage and the air-brakes.

Because of this, after a successful Flight 1 in September 1964 it had been grounded again for three further months to bring it up to a standard suitable for the full test programme.

This was where things began to happen! On Flight 3 an undercarriage sequence malfunction aborted the flight (*Picture 1 – page 118*) and after remedial action Flight 4 produced the same malfunction but on the other side (*Picture 2*).

The author takes a close look at the camera-Meteor in 1965 flying a Lightning 6 over the Lake District.

1 *TSR2 Flight 3. Port undercarriage failed to retract. The author and Don Bowen.*

2 *TSR2 Flight 4. Starboard undercarriage failed to retract. Crewed by the author and Don Bowen.*

3 *TSR2 Flight 5. Both legs failed to retract and then failed to de-rotate to the landing position. The author and Don Bowen.*

TSR2 flies past Boscombe tower for visual check of the undercarriage.

TSR2 on 'Finals' with the undercarriage not fully extended. Flight 5.

TSR2 touching down 'gently' with the wheels in the wrong place! Flight 5 Boscombe Down. Crewed by the author and Don Bowen.

The airloads were proving too great for the hydraulic rotation forces at the u/c bogeys, and these were 'hanging up' in the vertical position and refusing to rotate further into 'uplock'.

Luckily 'down' selection cleared this malfunction in the early flights enabling normal landings to be made and, after a lengthy period of further remedial engineering, Flight 5 occurred.

This time the failure was more comprehensive and potentially disastrous (*picture 3*)! The bogey beams had both reached equilibrium against the airloads and then refused to move further into 'uplock', or to 'downlock' when selected.

I could find no way to influence the situation and time was running out with the remaining fuel. This was a justifiable 'abandon-aircraft' case and I offered Don Bowen, the test observer, the 'Martin-Baker option'* which he declined with what I felt was considerable fortitude.

I then set about making the smoothest landing of my life, hoping that the already established precision of the elevator control of this heavy, fast aircraft, would permit a touch down sufficiently gentle to allow the u/c main wheels to rotate backwards (i.e. the wrong direction) into correct twin-wheel contact.

It is to the great credit of the aerodynamics and controls systems designers that this is exactly what happened when TSR2 touched down at a recorded six inches per second descent-rate, and then with gentle forward stick I was able to progressively unload the wing causing the aircraft to sink quite slowly on to its correct four-wheel attitude.

The prototype had been saved from destruction by airmanship as was widely acknowledged in the profession, although I knew that the quality of the elevator control had been a great help!

Before long the crew began to notice that no appreciation of this achievement, formal or otherwise, was forthcoming from any of the authorities involved, and there never was subsequently.

So it was all the more interesting to learn more than twenty years later from a retired member of the undercarriage design team that this potential fault had been identified and reported through the appropriate channel two years before the flight trials began!

The report (which I read in 1984) had been suppressed by BAC management and never circulated to the vitally involved 'Airworthiness' and 'Flight Operations' departments, and no corrective design action had been taken – but it was taken after Flight 5!

This was a classic example of breakdown in the essential cross-flow of information between specialist departments in the major co-ordination of a new design right through to Flight 1 and beyond.

It was in no way a failure of design itself because the potential hazard had been identified and reported correctly in good time. But it was a gross failure of management which could have had far-reaching and fatal consequences.

A failure which I am assured could not possibly happen today, but test-pilots should, I feel, check on that assurance from time to time!

---

* the Martin-Baker ejection seat.

Sir Dermot Boyle names the Lightning at Farnborough in 1958, with Lord Nelson of Stafford.

The author in the Lightning 6 development prototype on its first flight from Filton in 1964.

VIP flight. Air Minister Julian Amery with the author at Warton in 1961.

The author flying a Lightning 6 on test over the Lake District in 1965.

The TSR2 prototype just prior to exceeding Mach 1 for the first time during February 1965. Crewed by the author and Peter Moneypenny.

The Warton legacy. TSR2, Lightning 6 and Canberra B2.

Chapter Eight

Royal Occasion –
Flying King Hussein

Late on the evening of Friday 14 December 1965 Freddy Page called my home to say that I was wanted at Amman, the capital of Jordan, on the following Monday to fly a Lightning for King Hussein.

In our industry sudden events with scarcely enough time for preparation were quite normal, but this seemed a little marginal and I asked Freddy how we were going to get a Lightning to Amman in time. 'The Air Force are flying two in from Akrotiri [Cyprus],' he said, 'and you will need to be there by Sunday evening to see the British Ambassador.'

This all seemed to be becoming rather heavyweight and there was more to come, as I found later.

But in the absence of any further briefing information I made hasty travel arrangements, packed a bag and boarded the BOAC VC10 flight (for Sydney via Amman) on the Sunday afternoon.

As always it was a pleasant flight on the VC10 service in first class and shortly before the let-down to Amman with the sun already setting over Beirut, a small smartly dressed passenger with a dark, bushy moustache came down the aisle and saying 'Good evening,' sat down by me.

He didn't introduce himself, but began talking pleasantly in generalities before asking what was bringing me to Amman. I said that I was looking forward to my visit as I had been there before, and that I had commercial interests there.

He did not pursue this, wished me a pleasant visit and went back to his seat leaving me wondering who he was; but presently, as we all prepared to disembark, one of the stewardesses said 'Did you know that was Crown Prince Hassan you were talking with?' In view of my ignorance of any details of my visit I was glad that I had been reserved over his questions!

In a waiting car I was driven quickly to the British 'Residence' and ushered into a small room full it seemed with rather anxious people!

The Ambassador welcomed me briefly, saying that I would know most of the people there, and I saw Tom Prickett (Air Marshal Sir Thomas) C-in-C RAF Middle East, George Black (W/Cdr i/c Lightning conversion unit, Coltishall), and a retired soldier with a legendary reputation in desert warfare who just happened to be there.

The Ambassador came straight to the point. 'His Majesty is to fly the two-seat Lightning (T4) and after that he wants you to demonstrate the single-seater (F3).' This seemed straightforward, but then he said, 'There is a problem, the King wants you to fly him.'

This did not seem to be a problem either, but then I saw what was obviously in their minds. The Air Force had brought their Lightnings in on an official visit at 'Air Rank' level and they expected that any flying would be done by the RAF themselves, hence the presence of George Black for this purpose.

It was now approaching 1 a.m. and the King was timed to be at Amman airport at 8 a.m. I had not even seen Amman airport from the cockpit in daylight and I would have no chance to do so before taking off in the Lightning! There was also the matter of getting some sleep first.

While this was going through my mind no-one said anything, and so I waited. It seemed to be a very long silence and then the Ambassador said, 'The Air Force are not entirely happy that what they see as their responsibility should be taken over by a civilian!'

I said that in no sense was I there to 'take over' anything from the Air Force, but, as I saw it, it was also important not to offend the monarch so that there might have to be a compromise. The silence continued and I said, 'How would it be if I flew the Lightning demonstration and George Black flew the monarch in the T4?'

There were nods of agreement from Tom Prickett and George Black, but the Ambassador said, 'That leaves unanswered the question that Hussein has specifically asked for Beamont to fly him.' (I had had a pleasant audience with him a few months earlier in which we had talked at length about the Lightning.)

Here was the crunch point. It was clear that the buck was being passed to me, so I said 'Perhaps we should say to the King that, since George Black is the RAF's top instructor on Lightnings and in charge of Lightning flying training for the RAF, he would be the best pilot of all to fly the King as Beamont was a technical test pilot and not a qualified flying instructor.'

They could, of course, have said that for me but perhaps it hadn't occurred to them, and so it was arranged and in an atmosphere of unspoken relief we all retired for a few hours sleep.

Arriving at Amman airport at 7 a.m., with the early sun flooding the red Jordanian desert all around in pink and orange hues, I set about checking the Lightnings with our company representative, and then briefing on the airport, the surrounding flying area and rules and controls for my demonstration. George Black would of course obtain his own clearances for flying the King.

What had to be done was now professionally straightforward with the exception that it was going to be the first time I had done a low-level high-performance demonstration flight over an airfield (and country) that I had never seen before from the cockpit!

I was also conscious that King Hussein might not be pleased that his choice of the pilot for his flight had been refused.

He was not pleased, and it was immediately apparent when I went out to meet him that the explanation that had been given to him was that I did not want to fly him!

This was not developing into a happy event, but despite his clear displeasure I climbed up to the Lightning and helped him into the cockpit, checked his harness and his understanding of the ejector seat drill and then handed over to George Black saying, 'Have a good flight your Majesty'. With his famous graciousness and good manners and obviously eagerly anticipating what was to come he said, 'Thank you, I am looking forward to it'.

George took him straight into the Lightning's dramatic near-vertical climb from take-off and disappeared to the south over the red Jordan hills, demonstrating the controls and systems on their way to 30,000ft.

There the King took control as George lit the 'reheat' afterburners. The King accelerated to Mach 1.6 and then entered a supersonic turn back towards Amman at Black's request. But Hussein was enjoying himself and he soon turned away on a different heading. George said, 'Where are we going Sir?' and the King said, 'To see my wife!' and he flew the Lightning down to low level round the Summer Palace until George had to say, 'The fuel is getting low Sir'. They scraped back in to Amman with no reserves of fuel left. At least they had no difficulty in obtaining air traffic priority to land!

Then it was my turn and, with the King and party seated in comfortable chairs in front of the air traffic control building, I started up Lightning 3 XG735 and taxied out on to the strange aerodrome in the hot clear sunshine, and on ATC instructions 'Clear to back-track the Main,' I headed to the eastern end of the main runway.

Turning to line up for the westerly take-off I looked around at the sharply clear horizon which was bounded on all sides by barren and featureless red rolling hillsides.

The visibility was, in fact, so clear as to make distance judgement very difficult and I felt that this might be a problem in the forthcoming fast, high-G display routine.

Then it was time to go and with 'Lightning you are clear for six minute display,' I lit the reheats, and because of the high ambient temperature (35°C plus) stayed at maximum RH power for the first four minutes of aerobatics and very tight turns within the airfield boundary, controlling speed throughout not with throttle adjustment but by increasing or decreasing induced drag with back or forward stick as necessary – an effective technique which I had developed at many Farnborough displays and elsewhere.

It had the dramatic effect of the continuous roar of the reheated Avons, and more importantly it provided an effective counter to the inevitable thrust loss resulting from the high temperature of the day.

Completing with a throttled-back slow fly past along the display line at fifty feet in landing configuration, air-brakes out, I pulled the Lightning sharply up, banging in max. reheat again and rolling in a steep climbing turn back into the downwind leg for landing.

Little was said by the official party who were apparently still subdued by the Royal coolness when I climbed down from the cockpit, but the smiles on the faces of the RAF ground crews and their 'thumbs-up' showed the approval of those well-known severe critics of pilot technique!

But this enterprise did not end without some further embarrassment. While the flying was taking place the C-in-C's wife and daughter were shown the Royal Mews and seeing a beautiful Arab stallion the daughter exclaimed, 'What a lovely horse. I'd love to have him!' and, being a Royal guest, so she did!

This presented an urgent problem. How to take the gift-horse away. This was solved by an immediate order from the C-in-C to send his VIP Andover transport aircraft back to Amman after he and his party had flown home.

This was done and after removing most of the luxurious leather seating the horse was persuaded, much against his clearly expressed wishes, to enter the aircraft and be tethered for the short flight to Cyprus.

During this however the horse, clearly disenchanted with what was going on, expressed his disapproval by doing what horses do all over the luxurious interior all the way to Cyprus.

What the Akrotiri maintenance personnel thought about all this can be well imagined, but it came as no surprise to learn that the aircraft suffered such massive corrosion to its structure and systems that, it was said, it subsequently had to be written off and scrapped.

As a sales campaign it could not have been described as an unqualified success because, in the event, Jordan made the error of buying Lockheed F104 Starfighters on cut-price offer from the USAF; aircraft which proved to be seriously unsuitable for their major potential role of defence against the highly agile and sophisticated aircraft of the Israeli Air Force.

Lightnings would have suited the RJAF ideally at that period, but it was not to be.

W/Cdr George Black, the author, King Hussein and RJAF staff officers.

CHAPTER NINE

SAUDI ARABIAN LIGHTNINGS –
LIGHTNINGS FOR EXPORT

The great Saudi Arabian defence programme 'Al Yamamah' (that continues most successfully at the time of writing in its third decade), had its
beginnings in 1965 when English Electric, with the assistance of international arms salesman Geoffrey Edwards, challenged the established order in the
Middle East export field. Strong American missions were already in place in most
of the Arab states, capitalising on their dominance of oilfield technology in the
region.

In the vital absence of government support when it was most needed the
Lightning had so far failed to achieve export orders unlike its famously successful
predecessor, the Canberra; but now a major opportunity emerged.

While the air forces of the Western world and of the other major industrialised
nations had been equipped in recent years with fighters, and in some cases fighter-bombers, with supersonic performance, the rest of the world had not and
many countries had begun to see that they were at a serious military disadvantage
but could not afford the huge costs of the new technology.

Arabia on the other hand, had become the most prolific oil-producing area
outside the United States, and now the greatest producer, Saudi Arabia, found
itself threatened by its neighbours Iraq and Iran, both of whose air forces had
supersonic aircraft on order from the West.

The Royal Saudi Arabian Air Force (RSAAF) was a small, well-trained force
mainly equipped with outdated propeller-driven aircraft and was advised by a
resident in-country Pakistan Air Force mission; and now they were planning to
become a fully supersonic air force. This would demand a major reorganisation
and the Americans were already at Jeddah and Riyadh offering to supply aircraft,
support and all-through training facilities.

This had wide-ranging implications as the conversion of the Saudi Arabian
defence system from subsonic to supersonic would also involve massive restruc-
turing of their radar defences and training system, and would necessitate a wide
range of support activities. We learnt that the Americans were already planning
to demonstrate two supersonic types, the Northrop F1 and the Lockheed 104
Starfighter, at Riyadh in the very near future!

I knew that the 104 was much inferior as an air superiority defence fighter to
our Lightning, and that the Northrop was more an interim fighter trainer with
significantly less performance than the other contenders; but would the Saudis
appreciate this or see through the persuasive American sales presentations!

It seemed an immense and complicated task, but Lord Nelson decided that
English Electric would bid for it if supported by HMG. In the event, with

Lightning F53 for Saudia Arabia on test from Warton in 1967.

commendable foresight government support was made available, and in late 1965 specialists from Warton were dispatched to assess and evaluate the potential requirement. This proved to be formidable.

I sent Jimmy Dell out from Warton Flight Operations to evaluate the four main bases named for Lightning deployment; Riyadh, the capital's airport and headquarters of the RSAAF; Dhahran on the Arabian Gulf coast; Taif, newly developed in the north on the border with Israel at Eilat on the Red Sea; and Khamis Mushayt on the southern border of the Empty Quarter and within a few minutes by jet of Sana'a, the capital of hostile North Yemen.

Dell reported that all the airfields were well-sited and well-built, and that Riyadh and Dhahran had adequate hangarage, flight-line and administration accommodation, but that these facilities were not yet available though under development at Taif and Khamis.

He also pointed out that in the absence of all-weather aids on these airfields, approach radars would be a minimum requirement for Lightning operations.

Then, after a successful demonstration of a Lightning at Riyadh by Dell before the King and the service chiefs, it was soon confirmed that a massive programme was envisaged by the Saudi government involving approximately fifty Lightnings and a similar number of Strikemaster jet trainers developed from the Jet Provost with provision for ground-attack capability.

The author flying the first 'export' Lightning 53 for Saudi Arabia with Matra missile launchers. Warton in 1967.

The Saudis made it clear that the go-ahead for this major commitment would depend absolutely on the British being able to demonstrate willingness and ability to react quickly by making a token delivery of Lightnings within a short period.

There was only one way to do this of course and HMG, again with admirable foresight, released from the RAF six F Mk 2 Lightnings and two T4 Lightning two-seaters for English Electric to overhaul, refurbish (as F Mk 52s and T Mk 54s) and deliver to the RSAAF the quickest possible way.

This was done with dispatch, and the aircraft were delivered by in-flight refuelling from RAF Victor tankers, direct from Warton to Jeddah by a combined team of Warton test pilots and experienced RAF fighter pilots from the Lightning Conversion Unit.

The pre-flight check on the first Lightning 55 for Saudi Arabia. Samlesbury in 1967, by the author.

One Lightning had to make a precautionary diversion to Amman in Jordan due to an electrical defect and this was soon rectified and the Lightning flown on to Jeddah. The aircraft were then established at Riyadh which was to become the initial Lightning base under the command of the RSAAF King Faisal Air Academy (KFAA).

Here an initial training unit was established consisting of Lightning QFIs (Qualified Flying Instructors) seconded from the RAF and screened by my department at Warton for two-year attachments. They were well paid for this of course and there was no shortage of volunteers for 'Lightning flying in the Desert'!

Operational training came under the management of a pilot specifically selected for the task for his experience and qualities of leadership, Tony Winship, Wing Commander RAF at the Coltishall Lightning conversion unit.

His task at Riyadh was, in effect, the Lightning squadron commander, but employed as civilian 'advisers' neither he nor his pilots were required or permitted to take part in hostilities and they were not to use military titles. Their role was strictly training, although in due course varied interpretations were applied to this rule! But Tony Winship turned out to be a splendid choice for this critical role.

When the Lightning activity began I visited Riyadh to discuss the operation with the pilots after establishing contact with the KFAA, and to satisfy the Warton Board that the Saudi operation was sound and going to plan.

In the process I flew Lightnings over the desert from Riyadh, particularly to experience some of the extreme conditions that would be encountered in the programme, such as:

- Extreme heat on the ground which could easily result in skin burns from hot metal on unprotected hands or arms when climbing into cockpits.
- Take-offs and landings at Lightning speeds in the intense sun-glare and in the critical reduction in visibility in sudden, unpredictable local dust storms.
- Navigation over the largely featureless sand and red-earth desert for hundreds of miles in every direction.
- Judgement of distance in the intense glare in low-flying training at high speed.

Subsequent to these experiences it was interesting to hear the views of the enthusiastic QFIs and to establish excellent rapport with Tony Winship who was clearly about to become a key member of the Riyadh operation in the delicate task of, on the one hand disciplining the Lightning pilots in an environment that seemed to them to be almost entirely free of 'service' controls and limitations, while on the other creating confidence with the commandant KFAA in the conduct of the BAC contract.

In this respect it soon became evident that there was, in the Lightning training area, another potentially disruptive factor to be contended with that demanded tact, diplomacy and, where necessary which it often was, firmness. This was the close supervision by the Pakistan military mission whose offices were based at the KFAA in the same building as the Lightning instructors' and pupils' flight offices, and who lost no time in criticising these British activities and reporting adversely on them to the KFAA command.

Handling tests with bombs on a Saudi Arabian Lightning

Saudi Lightning 53 with external bombs and retracting rocket launchers at Warton in 1966.

It was never made clear if the PAF Mission's terms of reference permitted them to take an other-than-neutral position in their 'advice' to the Saudi authorities; nevertheless audiences with the Saudi Commandant with the Pakistan 'advising' officer at his side became a routine and frequent part of my responsibilities over the next few years.

Always preceded by a professional briefing by Tony Winship and when necessary by some of his pilots, these meetings were seldom difficult because the criticisms and 'problem areas' brought up at the KFAA were nearly always based on misunderstandings and misinterpretations, although there were some examples of clear attempts to discredit 'the contractor'.

But the meetings had the very positive effect of providing a regular forum for the exchange of views on progress and the identification of genuine difficulties on both sides, and so gave valuable impetus to progress.

Some limited Lightning training began within a few weeks when especially screened Saudi 'students' began flying with instructors in the T54 two-seaters. These were pilots with appropriate experience of the North American F86 Sabre transonic fighter, of which the RSAAF had two squadrons.

This activity resulted, as we had hoped, in a sharp rise in morale at Riyadh; and in parallel the formation and development of the support administration, a responsibility under subcontract of Airwork Services Ltd, proceeded satisfactorily at first.

The author landing the first Saudi T55 at Manston on its first flight in 1968.

Two Lightning T55s for Saudi Arabia at Warton in 1967. Delivery pilots Dell, Ginger and Ferguson with the author.

Then came a set-back. The Lightning instructors, all first-class RAF fighter pilots, had set the tone for their operations at Riyadh by demonstrating the Lightning's exceptional ability to climb nearly vertically immediately after every take-off. These take-offs were well within sight of the city of Riyadh itself, so that the daily vertical departures of their new supersonic fighters into the glaring sky became widely talked about.

Moreover the Lightnings were loudly proclaimed by their young Saudi pilots to be the 'world's finest fighters' – a view which our company and the RAF personnel were happy to support.

But then one day one of the instructors in a single-seat F52 'overcooked' his climb-out and encountered the well-known 'yaws' phenomenon when the wing stalled. Still almost vertical and with no time or height for the pilot to correct the stall, the Lightning rolled over and dived vertically for the ground which it impacted in seconds, but miraculously the pilot ejected with only split seconds of time for his parachute to develop before his feet hit the ground rather hard only a short distance from his Lightning's fireball on the desert!

He was unhurt, but he was not popular and was sent home forthwith. Meantime this was a critical event for so early in the contract.

There was no question about responsibility but there were obvious complications in the area of insurance. The company's managing director, Viscount Caldecote, gave assurances to the Saudi Minister of Defence, Prince Sultan, that there was no defect in the aircraft and that a replacement would be found; but here a difficulty occurred. The RAF had no further F Mk 2s to release for conversion to Mk 52 standard.

Meanwhile Warton had found that another aircraft could be built to the highest F Mk 53 standard, which would of course be a valuable addition to the main Lightning order and at significantly higher cost than the crashed F52. This, it was

A Saudi Mk 55 on its first flight from Samlesbury to Warton.

assumed, would be adjusted in due course.

However, when Lord Caldecote returned to Jeddah to inform Prince Sultan of Warton's proposal he said, 'Your Highness, we are delighted to say that we have found a replacement for your crashed Lightning,' and the Prince was graciously pleased and said, 'Thank you so much.' Robin Caldecote found that he had given the Saudis a brand new top-of-the-range Lightning costing millions, and that was going to come out of the profit!

There were no further major setbacks in the Lightning build-up period and, over the next year the complete force of fifty-three Lightnings was delivered by direct flights from Warton to Jeddah and Dhahran with RAF Victor tankers.

The flights were so regular and on time that at Jeddah International airport they were said to be more reliable than the airlines! Once again conducted by Warton test pilots and RAF squadron pilots, they were much sought after as great and enjoyable experiences, and each pilot received from the Saudi authorities a gold watch 'in appreciation' after the final direct stage to Dhahran.

A production Lightning 53 for Saudi Arabia ready for its first flight at Samlesbury in 1967.

The build-up to full Lightning training presented no serious operating problems, but there were long periods of crisis in the technical area resulting from the harsh conditions on the Gulf coast that were new to the Lightning. Intense heat combined with very high humidity and salt-laden air resulted in many severe corrosion problems. In particular in the engine starting system (Iso-Propyl Nitrate turbine starters) which came close to grounding the fleet before technical solutions were found and applied after urgent redesign effort and heroic endeavours by Warton's service department in the field.

There were many other problems that were tackled with resolution and resolved by Warton, and then a new extreme problem developed. The management in Saudi Arabia (by Airwork Services) of the administration and support programme for the contract had got into difficulties due to under-manning, resulting in the need for frequent visits by Warton management and engineering personnel to the Lightning bases just to keep the programme operating. This of course caused increasing friction between the companies, and increasing displeasure from the Saudi authorities.

My own regular meetings with the KFAA and periodic audiences with Prince Sultan, the Minister of Defence, which had always been conducted with firm authority but courtesy, now began to change tone with curt implications that the British were shortfalling on the contract becoming the order of the day.

This atmosphere was escalated by another event which came directly into my court. Reports were received that the Saudis were displeased with the standard of preparation of the first Strikemaster Jet Trainers that we had just delivered, and said they were 'incapable of carrying out the specified ground-attack role'.

This was serious and also mysterious because the Strikemaster was a simple aircraft and its weapons system as agreed under the contract was rudimentary but adequate for its purpose, so I was dispatched by the Board to investigate.

On arrival at Riyadh I learned from our headquarters that one of the Airwork-employed Strikemaster instructors had apparently been reporting directly to the Saudis with his opinions on the aircraft's 'inadequacies'. This action was of course irregular as his reporting channel, contractually clear, was through his head of department and specifically not to the customer.

Arriving at the KFAA the next morning where I had expected to talk firstly with the Strikemaster CFI, I was surprised to find the crew-room filled with the instructors, students and a Pakistan 'adviser', and to be told that the meeting would be chaired by a Strikemaster QWI (Qualified Weapons Instructor) who, it soon became apparent, was the source of the complaints!

Quickly deciding that to cancel the meeting would have precisely the wrong effect, I agreed with the arrangement and then listened with astonishment to a harangue accusing BAC (the parent corporation), English Electric, the constructors, and apparently Warton Flight Operations (i.e. myself) of gross incompetence and dishonesty in delivering aircraft to the RSAAF which were incapable of carrying out their 'weapons system role'.

When he seemed to have finished I said, mainly for the benefit of the Saudis present, that I was unable to recognise his difficulties and that I wanted to see them demonstrated. 'When?' he said. 'Right now,' I said. 'Clear us on to the

Range and we'll look at it together.'

The weapons range, about fifty miles out in the desert, was speedily made available and I went out with the Airwork instructor to one of the Strikemasters in the grilling midday heat (about 50°C), which was noticeably warm to this visitor straight out from a grey, cold and wet UK.

He indicated that I should take the right seat with him in command in the left seat, but I declined saying that I was 'current' on Strikemasters and more accustomed to the command seat, and that he could show me his 'problem' from his normal 'instructor's' position.

His manner which had been distinctly hostile in the meeting room was now becoming even more so, and when I took off and cleared the Riyadh circuit climbing to ATC's specified 2000ft for transit to the range he suddenly said, 'We don't fly like this – I've got her,' and grabbing the controls he pushed over into a dive towards the desert floor.

Then he said, 'You people think you know about low flying at Farnborough etc. – I'll show you how it is done out here!'

He held the Strikemaster in a forty-five degree dive at 250kt until it was about to impact the desert and then, jerking the stick back at the very last moment levelled at less than fifty feet.

It immediately became apparent that what had previously appeared to be flat, scrub-patched, yellow sand and red and black rock-strewn desert ahead was now deeply uneven with undulating dunes tipped with bleak and rocky outcrops 20–50ft high.

The latter now became his targets as he flew down at each one to lift a wing over at what hopefully was the last moment. During one of these manoeuvres I looked back and saw that we were being followed by an immense plume of desert dust raised by the Strikemaster's turbulent wake at only a few feet above the ground!

What had been a professional but rather boring assignment had now become less than boring.

It was clear that the man on my right was in some sort of mental state and had decided to teach this 'visiting brass' a lesson he would not forget; and that indeed was about all he achieved that day.

While all this was going on with rocky outcrops appearing dead ahead in the windscreen or flashing by under the wing-tips at a bewildering rate, my instinct said 'grab the controls and pull up'. This was what he clearly wanted me to try, but in these extreme circumstances it was more than likely that he would grab the controls from me and push back down – a situation which would result in instant oblivion. So I did nothing.

With hands apparently relaxed (I hoped) on my knees I remained silent and just let him get on with it, knowing very well that we might at any moment be killed but also that if I showed any emotion at all he would regard it as victory.

So I said nothing and did not respond at all when he suddenly said, 'One of our students was doing this one day when he saw an Arab on top of a rock like that one ahead, and hit her (it was a woman) with his wing-tip, chopping off her head!' He seemed to think that funny.

By this time, as we skimmed past the rock I had realised that if we survived he would have to pull up to a safe height when we reached the range, and after that I could take over safely when necessary.

After an age (it was a few minutes only), a red flag appeared on the dunes ahead and then a line of square targets. He pulled up vertically – there was nothing smooth about this pilot – and he said, 'Well, what now?'

I said 'Carry on and demonstrate the problem,' and then regretted it as he predictably dived onto one of the targets pulling out so low that the top edge of the target was still visible in my windscreen just before we scraped over it. But I had noticed something else and I said, 'Do that again.'

On his next pass in the slightly turbulent air, my gunsight again showed that he was 'snaking' and not tracking the target accurately and then I saw that his feet were 'tramping' the rudder pedals.

His criticism of the 'system' had been that the Strikemaster could not deliver weapons to the contract accuracy, so I said 'I've got her' and set up a standard bombing attack, followed by a shallower 'guns' attack, each time finding the desert turbulence distracting. But it was easily possible to eliminate 'snaking' during the aiming phase by gentle and not 'tramping' rudder corrections.

He could, of course, see through his gunsight that in my passes the aiming spot was steady on target each time for long enough for a guns burst or bomb release.

I said 'Anything else you want to show me' and he muttered something like, 'It's no bloody good,' so I flew back to Riyadh, this time enjoying the desert scenery from a comfortable 500ft until rejoining the Riyadh circuit at the prescribed 2000ft.

I reported my findings to the Commandant KFAA who accepted them without comment, and no more was heard of this.

After his attempt to discredit BAC the Airwork pilot was sent home of course, and shortly after that I had the task of screening the remaining Strikemaster contract instructors, finding two more who did not have their contracts renewed. Thereafter BAC pilot morale at Riyadh and at the Lightning stations returned to its required high level and was a major factor in the success of the long-term programme.

It was odd that in a long flying life which had not been without a few exciting moments, that episode had been one of my closest shaves!

But following this further disruption, the deterioration in the Airwork management system eventually resulted in the Saudi government demanding that English Electric Warton (BAC) should take over all responsibility from Airwork or else the whole British Contract, technical and administrative, would be cancelled and the defence programme handed to the Americans.

This presented an enormous challenge with need for immediate and drastic expansion at Warton, and our view expressed to HMG was that this would be practical only if the contract responsibility was assumed by HMG who would then subcontract the management to Warton. This was effected remarkably quickly, and the challenge was met by setting up an entirely new Saudi Management facility at Warton together with strengthened administration at Riyadh, which quickly became most successful and has maintained professional and profitable control of what has become acknowledged over more than thirty years as Britain's largest-ever export programme with potential for many more successful years to come.

This was one of the achievements of the hard-pressed, capable, loyal and determined Warton team in the late 1960s and early 1970s.

The eighth development Lightning Mk1, XG 313 (1st flight RPB 2.2.59) testing 2″ RPs in the spring of 1960.

Chapter Ten

Lightnings strike twice

The terms of reference for the expatriate pilots in the Saudi Arabian defence programmes 'Magic Carpet', 'Magic Palm' and the ultimate long-term 'Al Yamamah' included at the insistence of HMG, '. . . .for training duties only and not to take part in armed military operations of any kind'.

This would only become relevant in the unlikely event of hostilities affecting the Kingdom, but it was felt that these experienced instructors would, in fact, find themselves in a sensitive situation if hostilities were to break out.

However the programme progressed year after year with pupils being screened from the desert and from the Royal Palaces and then put through English language training, basic and jet transition flying training; and ultimately through Lightning training to fully qualified and able squadron operational standard. It was a major success, and after a decade or more it was seen as stable with potential need for many more years of support and also the major possibility of further extensions in the future with new equipment (the Tornado).

The operation in the desert had been made a significant British Export success, and then came a de-stabilising moment.

Without apparent intelligence warning the southern border of the Kingdom came under invasion by a strong armoured force from North Yemen which thrust from the Sana'a area out into the Empty Quarter in the general direction of the capital Riyadh.

It had not been thought practical for a threat to develop in that area due to the extreme conditions of the Empty Quarter, but nevertheless after only two days the North Yemenis had penetrated more than 100 miles and were seen to be posing a threat to Riyadh only 200 miles of empty desert away.

The Saudi army, caught off guard, were unable to mount any significant counter forces and the RSAAF were immediately in action on reconnaissance and limited ground-attack missions. Meanwhile Tony Winship had reported the Lightning squadrons at Readiness, and they were ordered to Khamis Mushayt for 'air cover operations' against possible (but improbable) MiG operations from Yemen. Winship proposed use of the Lightnings to strike the 'head of the column' while they were still in range. He said that ground attack with the 30mm Aden Cannons and 2-inch spin-stabilised rockets could be very effective (although the 2-inch rockets had never been used or envisaged for use in this role).

The Commander-in-Chief RSAAF with the entire responsibility for stopping the invasion on his hands, quickly gave authority and Winship led the Lightnings to Khamis Mushayt where, with enthusiastic and professional support by BAC and RSAAF personnel, refuelling and arming-up were completed quickly. Then the Lightning squadron took off for the Empty Quarter led by Tony Winship on his own initiative.

Finding the target hundreds of miles into the barren desert was no problem, Winship said later, as the armoured vehicles and trucks of the Yemeni force left deep tracks in the empty sand which could be seen from any altitude and followed for many miles ahead!

These tracks led to where the enemy had laagered in a fortified village, and the Lightnings attacked with devastating effect using rockets and cannon fire. There was what was described as 'some impressive return fire', but not for long.

With all returning safely to Khamis Mushayt, Winship reported favourably on the Lightning's ability in ground attack, and he was ordered out again at first light next day.

On this sortie they found the Yemenis in the same place, possibly unable to move because of the previous day's attack.

So, attacking again Winship was able to gain a clear assessment of the use of the spin-stabilised rockets – a weapon rejected by the RAF due to low accuracy air-to-air, but never tried by them air-to-ground.

Winship reported that they were very effective fired from short range (about 700yd) and that they appeared to have knocked out a lot of vehicles.

Returning from this sortie one of the Lightnings reported hydraulic failure and was losing flying controls. Winship ordered him to eject 'and stay by your parachute'.

The Saudi pilot, a member of the Royal Family, did this and Winship marked his landing before heading back with the formation for Base.

There, with remarkable organisation, the RSAAF launched a C130 Hercules with an armed rescue team, and Winship led them back to the scene.

The Saudi pilot was located by sighting his parachute, and the next phase of this remarkable operation began when the C130 transport Saudi captain, experienced in desert operations, made the courageous and very high-risk decision to land on the rough desert floor nearby.

Bringing this off successfully, the Lightning pilot was rescued and flown back to Khamis Mushayt unhurt.

There the lines of communication had been incandescent all day, and when Tony Winship reported for his next operations order he was told, 'You can stand down – through intermediaries at Amman the South Yemenis have called for a cease-fire!' The Lightnings had caused such destruction apparently that the strikes had immobilised and defeated the invading force!

When the dust had settled two things became clear.

The Commander-in-Chief of the RSAAF had defeated the Kingdom's enemies without help from the Army, but with much help from his Lightning force!

And Tony Winship had some explaining to do about how he and some of his pilots became involved in hostilities!

It was quite simple, he said. The 2-inch spin-stabilised rockets had never been used against ground targets. As the Lightning 'adviser' it was clearly his responsibility to investigate their use and make recommendations!

As contractors we received no formal report on this operation or on any political outcome, but over the months and years ahead it became apparent that Tony Winship was held in high regard by the Saudi authorities, and it was said that thereafter he used to return each year to the UK to buy a new yacht!

The author's last Lightning test flight. Jimmy Dell, Chief Test Pilot, the author and Freddy Page (MD). 1968.

The last production Lightning 6 with Managing Director Freddy Page and the author at Warton in 1968.

Chapter Eleven

Training for Concorde

In late 1964 an urgent call to my office at the English Electric Company's headquarters airfield at Warton in Lancashire requested my presence at Weybridge to see Sir George Edwards, managing director of the then new British Aircraft Corporation and of Vickers Supermarine.

This meant making time from my responsibilities for the Lightning development programme and, concurrently, technical preparation for the coming TSR2 testing.

So I flew down to Wisley and was driven immediately to Sir George's office at the Brooklands Vickers works.

In his traditionally direct way he came straight to the point. 'Jock (Bryce) is retiring immediately on health grounds,' he said.

He did not need to frame the next question. Jock Bryce had been appointed Chief Test Pilot of the new (BAC) corporation as, Sir George had said, Jock had the necessary experience of civil airliner requirements that, he perceived, would be the main business of BAC for the foreseeable future. Many people at the Military Aircraft Division at Warton and elsewhere had doubted this.

At the same time, in accepting the contract for the military TSR2 programme BAC had appointed me its project pilot as Deputy Chief Test Pilot, because, to use the words of my English Electric Chief Freddy Page (Sir Frederick Page CBE), 'there was no-one at Vickers with suitable supersonic flight test experience . . .'

It might have been put more graciously, but as it would be an interesting project and a privilege to be responsible for the next strike aircraft for the RAF, I got on with it!

But now here was a new situation – who was to take overall charge of the Corporation's test flying from Jock Bryce; and that would also mean who was to take on the flight test programme for Concorde?

As I was the Corporation's 'deputy' it was not for me to question the position, so I waited for Sir George. He looked out of the window and then back at me and said, 'Well, who is going to do the Concorde?'

It was not clear whether this was a rhetorical question or whether I was being offered the job, so I said that the Mach 2.0/500KIAS/60,000ft flight envelope and 'Delta' characteristics of the Concorde were comfortably within my experience and that I would enjoy doing it, but that I would need to recruit an experimental test pilot with experience of airline requirements to form a balanced team.

Sir George nodded and said, 'Do you want Concorde?' Thinking quickly I said yes but that there had to be some other considerations. My current commitments needed all my time and effort and adding a major new task would require adjustments somewhere. For example, while the idea of being Chief Test Pilot

Concorde and in parallel Chief Test Pilot TSR2 was attractive and would be a unique experience, pragmatic consideration suggested that the delegation which would be essential in such an arrangement would most probably result in less than a total focus on each, and that TSR2 should probably remain my priority project for this reason for the next four years. This was a defining point in one's own career of course.

Then 'How about Trubshaw?' said Sir George. I said that he would be an excellent and natural choice, but that he would need to gain some experience and knowledge of supersonics. The conversation ended there without, I noted, any reference to who was now to assume Jock Bryce's title of Corporation CTP.

The decision was not long in coming however. Brian Trubshaw was appointed BAC Chief Test Pilot and he made a fine and successful job of the Concorde programme, eventually being advanced to a directorship on the BAC/British Aerospace main Board.

I continued to preside over the TSR2 test programme as Warton's Chief of Flight Operations and my BAC 'Deputy CTP' title just faded away and was not referred to again. I experienced some interesting test flying with the TSR2 until its political cancellation in 1965, but my brief contact with the Concorde programme did not end there!

The Guild of Air Pilots, of whom I was (and am) a Liveryman and Master Air Pilot, had in 1965 formed a Supersonic Transport Committee to review and advise on operational matters and in particular on training philosophy. This committee was composed almost entirely of senior Comet and Boeing 707 airline captains and was chaired by a serving RAF Wing Commander with experience only of Canberras. Supersonic experience was absent and I was invited to provide this aspect.

The journey from my Lancashire base to the Guild in London for periodic two-hour meetings was time-consuming, but it was an important subject and I attended whenever possible. But it very soon became apparent that the committee was far from impartial and had developed a surprising mind-set. The Concorde, said the airline captains, was just another aircraft and would require no special training other than for specific controls and navigation systems.

This view was unprofessional in the extreme and a long way wide of the mark and could, if not quickly corrected, have led to serious consequences in the introductory period of the world's first supersonic airliner into the airlines; and there was a precedent for this concern.

I cited the record of the introductory experiences of 'the first big jets' during which a number of serious incidents had occurred in the airlines with Boeings losing control in 'compressibility', and I quoted a report by the Flight Safety Foundation (USA) of December 1966 which said:

> 'No clear and precise instructions on how to recover from a high Mach dive appear to have been given to airline pilots . . . Airline pilots are unlikely at present to have much first-hand experience of the handling qualities of their aircraft at speeds above M_{mo} (Mach max. operating) and it is felt to be most important that, at the very least, they should be told what to expect and be advised how to cope with the situation should it ever occur.'

And in one major step the Concorde was going to more than double the performance of the Boeings!

In a surprising move from experienced professionals the Guild Technical Committee reacted abrasively and claimed that I was criticising the earlier Comet training programme which they said had been conducted professionally.

I had no reason to dispute this and pointed out that I had not been referring to the Comet programme but to the Boeing 707 introduction.

The Committee remained obdurate and as it became clear that I was wasting my time, I resigned; and shortly afterwards received a letter of fulsome regrets and thanks for my contributions!

But it did not end there – suddenly the Press published an extraordinary story saying that I was in dispute with the Air Secretary, Lord Shackleton, about the need for providing supersonic training for Concorde! It transpired that the Guild PR man had 'leaked' an internal confidential memorandum to the Press which I had addressed to the Supersonic Transport Committee, with no authority whatsoever!

I went to see Lord Shackleton who showed only concern about the subject matter and dismissed the 'leak' as of little importance. I explained my position in detail and was thanked for this.

The Master of the Guild of Air Pilots, Sir Dermot Boyle, was of course embarrassed and asked me if I thought he should write to the Air Secretary, but I suggested that as I had expressed his concern and my own to Lord Shackleton, perhaps a letter from the Clerk-to-the-Guild to Lord Shackleton's office explaining the lapse and the actions taken would suffice.

Shortly after that I received a letter from the Guild Secretary saying that Sir Dermot would have a formal letter of apology sent to me if I wished, and I replied with thanks but said that I did not want to be the cause of any further embarrassment!

I had been advocating strongly the provision of supersonic experience in Lightnings for selected Concorde airline pilots and test pilots, and this was the point disputed by Lord Shackleton on advice from his staff.

At this point Dr Russell of Bristol Aeroplane Co., BAC's designers with the French of the Concorde, wrote to Lord Shackleton saying that training on Lightnings would have no relevance to the Concorde programme as, he said, there were no significant similarities between the types; and he added that his pilot, Trubshaw, agreed. I began to wonder about my recommendation to Sir George Edwards!

It was not very long however before Dr Russell changed his mind and wrote to the Ministries saying that some Lightning experience might after all be useful if Lightnings could be provided!

The Master of the Guild then asked if I could help, and with the agreement of Freddy Page I established the possibility of giving some limited Lightning supersonic experience to selected airline pilots and Concorde test pilots at Warton. Jimmy Dell and I would do the flying in a Mk 5 Lightning two-seat trainer on loan from the Ministry.

But nothing more was heard of this until in 1967 I was interested to read in

Flight magazine that the Ministry had announced that supersonic experience would be provided at Boscombe Down in RAF Lightnings for selected airline pilots – and BAC Concorde test pilots! It had not been an entirely wasted effort.

That was my last connection with the fabulous Concorde until 1988 when the British Airways Concorde Flight most kindly flew me to Washington/Miami and back watching the whole operation from the training captain's check-seat behind the captain, except when slipping back into the cabin for periodic champagne and caviar – an altogether enjoyable experience and the best 'Free Lunch' I ever had!

Chapter Twelve

Finis

1978 turned out to be a rather exceptional year.

It was my thirty-first year with 'The Company' and they had all been packed with interest and the gathering momentum of achievement. Being part of the country's most successful post-war aviation design team had been hugely satisfying, with new challenges every year and always clear targets to aim for. Our record of successes had been formidable and the envy of many elsewhere in the shrinking aircraft industry.

My part in these activities did not seem to diminish, but on the contrary I was charged with interesting new responsibilities every year without losing any of the earlier ones!

By the middle 1970s as a director of the Warton Division of British Aerospace I was responsible for:

1. Flight Operations/Flight Testing, Airfield Management and Air Traffic Control at Warton and Samlesbury airfields.
2. Flight Test Engineering.
3. Divisional Publicity/Public Relations.
4. Industrial security (contingency planning for strike activities).
5. Saudi Arabian 'Al Yamamah' flight operations, training and aircrew recruiting.
6. Director Flight Operations Panavia Gmbh, for the international testing of the Tornado for the RAF and NATO air forces.

At one stage I was even asked to take over on an urgent basis, the in-country management of the BAC programme in Saudi Arabia which was by then in administrative crisis, as Director of Operations. For this I was apparently required to be based in Riyadh, and to continue to conduct all my other responsibilities by commuting to the UK, Germany and Italy as necessary in a 125 business jet which (with crew) would be put at my disposal.

It was I suppose a flattering offer, but sober reflection showed clearly that something, somewhere, would have to be off-loaded, and when I suggested this the answer was 'no'! So I did not accept the Saudi proposal and continued as before to discharge my BAC and Panavia responsibilities from my offices at Warton and Munich until the following year when the scene was changed dramatically.

In the summer of 1978 without prior warning or discussion I learnt at a Warton board meeting that NAMMA, the German government management organisation of the Panavia Tornado programme, had announced dissatisfaction with the conduct of the Panavia 'Flight Operations Panel', apparently on the grounds, they said, that it showed bias towards the 'British interest'.

This was my 'Panel' of course, and for five years of strenuous effort I and the British and other members of my international team had maintained a positive and, we believed, successful atmosphere of international impartiality in this work, though we had sometimes been criticised by the British side for not favouring them enough!

Nevertheless I was told that the NAMMA general manager, retired Luftwaffe General Bechenbeil, was demanding my removal from the BAe Warton Board as a condition for my remaining in charge of Panavia Flight Operations.

I could hardly believe this, but when I pointed out that this could also be taken to mean that I would have to resign from Panavia if I was to retain my position and responsibilities at Warton, I was told that this was not how my old chief Freddy Page, by now Sir Frederick, Chief Executive of British Aerospace, saw it. He, I was told (not by him) wished me to relinquish all Warton responsibilities and continue with Panavia, thereby giving in entirely to the German pressure.

After my thirty apparently rather successful years at Warton I could not believe that this was happening, and so I asked to see the Chief Executive (Page).

A lunch was arranged at Brown's Hotel in London and I flew down with Page's replacement at Warton, the new chairman.

Over lunch they maintained a detailed discussion on a corporation administrative matter until over the coffee Page said, 'Well, I've another appointment,' at which point I raised the matter which I thought we had come down for.

Page said with some impatience, 'We've been through all that' (which I certainly had not). 'Bechenbeil wants you off the Warton Board and that is the way it has to be.' Then he departed with no reference to our thirty years of close association and of my loyal support through good times and bad, or of any regret at this somewhat traumatic situation.

I just could not believe that an official of the German government could instruct the chief executive of a major British business on how to manage his corporation and be allowed to get away with it!

In the aircraft going back to Warton I said to the chairman that this situation could also imply that I was being seen as redundant at Warton, and I asked what compensation had they in mind. He replied, 'You would be advised not to pursue that line as it could have an adverse affect on your final pension.'

It was not easy to discuss all this with Pat who of course had a good idea that something was badly wrong, but she was as always at her strongest and most supportive in the bad times. There had been many in our long and wonderful marriage, but this proved to be one of the hardest.

With indecent haste no time was given for reflection or further discussion and, during a Warton Board meeting that occurred next day, Les Trueman, the Company Secretary, came in, apologised to the Chair and put a paper in front of me saying 'You need to sign this today . . .'

'This' turned out to be my resignation from the Warton Board – just that with no elaboration.

I left the meeting telling my colleagues that it would seem to be my last with them (after thirteen years on the Board) and I returned to my office where I dictated to my loyal and incredulous secretary, Chrys Butcher, a memorandum to Sir Frederick Page saying that I would only resign my Warton directorship on the understanding that I would take early retirement from both BAe and Panavia no more than twelve months from that date, and that this would complete my part in the Tornado programme.

Page responded immediately by saying that my retirement would not be before the actual entry into service with NATO of the first series-production Tornado. He clearly did not want that boat to be rocked!

It was by now penetratingly clear that Page and some of the people whom I had regarded as warm and respected colleagues, were set on conceding to the German demand without personal discussion with me and there was absolutely nothing I could do about it!

I did consider the remaining option of resigning all my posts in British Aerospace and Panavia immediately, but at age fifty-seven that would have endangered my pension and left Pat and my family with no means of support – and I still had this now apparently idiotic ideal of loyalty to my old company and to the NATO Tornado.

So there was no other recourse. I resigned from the Warton Board, and then continued to run the Munich-based Tornado testing programme for another year with no noticeable change in attitude or increase in helpfulness from my German colleagues. The change may have satisfied their national ambitions but it made no difference at all to the efficient running of the Tornado testing programme.

The first series-production Tornado was delivered to NATO in July 1979, and I left my office at Warton for the last time on 1 August.

I found it difficult to believe what had happened and felt that I did not really understand why.

Twenty years later I had still received no explanation; but in June 1998 the Chief Executive of the British Aerospace Corporation (as it had evolved from BAC) which was by then virtually the whole British aircraft industry, sent his plushest 125 business jet to fly me to Warton for a day of personal briefing on the Eurofighter/Typhoon (which I would have dearly loved to fly!), and over lunch he presented me with a splendid painting of my all-time favourite, an English Electric Lightning, suitably inscribed.

I think someone was sending me a message.

Chapter Thirteen

How They Flew

Aeroplanes are designed to meet specific requirements; for airliners runway performance, range, payload, passenger comfort and commercial competitiveness; and for military aircraft, performance, weapons and weapon systems capability, and for some the ability to operate when necessary from restricted 'tactical' airstrips.

They are seldom designed specifically to please pilots, but throughout the history of aviation there has never been a successful aircraft seriously disliked by its pilots; on the contrary the accolade 'a pilot's aeroplane' generally means success for the type, as does 'a driver's car' in the world of motoring.

In the forty years from 1939 I had the good fortune to experience 180 different types of aircraft, an activity often described as 'type-hogging' by pilots less inclined to get off their backsides unless ordered to fly something! The more I flew the more fascinated I became with the varied characteristics I encountered and the qualities which went into making aircraft good, exceptional or unacceptable from the pilot's point of view.

In relation to this range of experience the question is frequently raised, 'What was your favourite aircraft?' There is no simple answer of course.

There have been a number that really stood out from the crowd, but each in its own period and in relation to a specific type of operation.

Looking back at the aircraft flown in training, Tiger Moths, Harts and Harvards were sound and straightforward; although I never really enjoyed the Tiger Moth then or since, but it did its job.

Then the Hurricane. It was awesome for a nineteen-year-old to sit solo behind 1000hp of Rolls-Royce Merlin, with those clean monoplane wings enclosing no fewer than eight machine-guns with which I would have to fly into close combat with enemy aircraft, and probably very soon as we were at war and my posting to a squadron was imminent.

But then I began to appreciate, as training flying progressed, that this famous fighter was so well-mannered, responsive and easy to fly and particularly to land, that it soon became an enthralling pleasure.

Before I had time to learn all its qualities my posting came to 87 Fighter Squadron at Lille Séclin in the British Expeditionary Force in France in November 1939. It was fortunate for me and the other just-out-of-training pilots that the major shooting war had not yet started, and that there would hopefully be valuable time for squadron training until the spring.

As a taste of things to come however, 87 Squadron had shot down a reconnaissance Heinkel 111 near Lille just before my arrival and the spirit in the squadron was tremendous.

Then in the intense fighting which began on 10 May 1940 and continued with increasing intensity over the Channel in June and July, and again in the Luftwaffe's major assault on the RAF over the South of England and London in August and September, we all learnt that our Hurricanes could bore in against intense defensive fire and destroy Dorniers, Heinkels and Ju 88s with responsive and accurate controllability and fine, steady gun-aiming.

Then when Me 110 twin-engined fighters intervened we could see them off easily in turning combat, although they had more speed in the dive and could get away if we did not hit them first time!

The high Bf 109 protective screen was generally broken up by our marvellous Spitfire 'top cover' but not always of course, and then our Hurricanes could easily out-turn the attacking Messerschmitts and nail them if they stayed turning! The Bf 109s could however always out-dive and out-climb us.

It was a hard battle that summer with heavy losses on both sides, but we felt that we were winning and we had immense confidence in our Hurricanes.

Every sortie in my 'LK-L' was a joy tempered by some apprehension as we climbed out over the coast to find out what was going to happen today! But joy redoubled at how well she had coped over Portland or wherever, and then came difficulty in refraining from an officially discouraged 'Victory Roll' at ridiculously low altitude over our squadron 'Dispersal'!

Despite the fierceness of the battle that summer we enjoyed our Hurricanes so much that we continued, often even after a day's fighting, to take off in the late evening for fifteen minutes 'Formation Aeros'!

The team of three, Ian Badger and the writer led by our irrepressible Flight Commander Derek Ward, was kept in being (by our replacement COs as first one, then another was killed) right on until the victory in October, as an undoubted morale booster for all personnel.

So confident were we in our Hurricanes that this activity was continued with impressive success into full night formation aerobatics in the winter of 1940/41.

I continued to fly Hurricanes in 87 and 79 Squadrons until November 1941 when, at the end of a two-year Tour I was posted 'on rest' to the Hawker Company to test Hurricanes off the Langley production line. This was a busy time, and on one day my log-book records eleven test flights between 9 a.m. and 4 p.m!

In all this I had acquired an affinity with my Hurricane. It had never let me down and had given me an immense feeling of confidence in combat, and also in the most atrocious weather – it could land safely in adverse conditions that would completely defeat a Spitfire.

I enjoyed its stable precision and its ability to hold tighter formation drill than we ever saw anywhere else. In working up our formation aeros team Derek Ward had demanded that our wing-tip overlap should be between his wing-tip and tailplane.

Being a dutiful officer I did as I was bid – and then bumped his tailplane! We both landed safely with minor damage, and he said, 'I didn't mean that close!' or words to that effect.

During the later war years a loud lobby of Spitfire protagonists began to proclaim to anyone who was gullible enough to listen to them that the Spitfire was superior in every way to the 109 and to the Hurricane in the Battle of Britain.

It was not of course. Each of these fighters had qualities which were superior to the others, and also characteristics which were inferior.

The Mks I and II Spitfires won the high-altitude battle without question, but the Hurricane was superior in close combat below 20,000 where most of the fighting took place.

The Spitfire lobby has escalated in the post-war years, egged on by the enthusiasm of some ancient pilots, amateur historians, air display freaks, and all those who confuse the sheer beauty of line of all Spitfires with operational effectiveness and capability. It was by no means always the most effective fighter, but the Spitfire will probably go down in history as the most beautiful military aircraft of all time, along with the Concorde as the civil contender.

But I enjoyed every minute of my 800 sorties in Hurricanes, and it was certainly my favourite in 1940!

Throughout 1941–44 I was able to fly most of the Spitfire developments which kept those lovely fighters generally on a par with their competitors in the Luftwaffe, and of these the Mk IX was possibly the overall best fighter above 30,000 until 1944 when the Griffon-engined Mk XIV became available to just about match the FW 190D (Dora).

At low level the Hawker heavy fighter, the Typhoon, was difficult to develop, but had great performance and ground-attack potential which it eventually demonstrated with great effect in 1944. Meanwhile a 'Typhoon II' development showed great promise and by 1944 this new fighter, now named Tempest V, came into service just in time to operate over the Normandy invasion and very soon after, in the intense battle for London against the Fieseler V1 flying bombs.

Having been involved in the Tempest's testing I had been impressed by its excellent handling, unusual accuracy in gun aiming, and high speed. It could not match the Spitfires above 20,000ft but below that its dive speed of 545mph and max. level of 415mph at 1000ft were not matched by any other conventional fighter at that time, including the Luftwaffe's best, the FW 190 which I had also flown and much enjoyed.

So it was with enthusiasm that I took the Tempests into action that summer with early successes against ground targets, and against Bf 109G6s two days after the beginning of the Invasion in Normandy.

The Tempests had easily caught and then out-turned in combat three Bf 109G6s out of a formation and destroyed them all.

Then from June to the end of August the Tempests had proved themselves to be far superior to any other type in destroying V1s, the Newchurch Wing scoring 638 on its own account.

I had found the Tempest to be not only an extremely effective 'tactical' (ground attack) fighter but superior in air combat and extremely efficient against the V1s. This latter required intensive all-day and part night operations in whatever weather the V1s were coming in, and demands on the pilots were severe.

In fact, in those summer months the morale in the Tempest squadrons rose to a remarkable level. The pilots enjoyed and were proud of their new fighters and of their successes, and for my part I was now enjoying this brilliant, precise and accurate aeroplane for the sheer pleasure of flying it. As had been the Hurricane in 1940, the Tempest was my favourite in 1944.

In the immediate post-war year there was an upheaval in aircraft development. The jet era had arrived but in America, France, Britain and Russia the first fighters to emerge with jet engines were a disappointment.

None of them had acceptable combat controllability, or in most cases even performance, to match the Me 262 jet fighter that entered the Luftwaffe in 1944 and which, had it not been for Hitler's misguided instruction to employ it as a ground-attack bomber, could have severely threatened the Allies' air attack over Germany in the last year of the war.

The Me 262 was potentially a brilliant fighter, with limiting Mach No. of 0.86 in 1944 which was not matched in service in this country until the Canberra in 1949–50.

I had been involved in testing the de Havilland Vampires and the early Meteors, and neither of these had inspired great affection. The Vampire was a pleasant aerobatic and easy aeroplane with its tricycle undercarriage, but its very short range and persistent low gun-platform stability and low Mach limits did not inspire great affection.

The Meteor was in a different category. I had flown one of the first (616) Squadron aircraft at Manston in the summer of 1944 and had been underimpressed. The jets were impressively smooth of course, although from the start of its long and ponderous take-off run it seemed very underpowered. The tricycle undercarriage was pleasant though.

Once airborne there were two immediate impressions. At full throttle the build-up of speed was very, very slow, while at the same time the build-up of control forces was becoming very noticeable and heavy. At its maximum speed low-down of about 485mph it was faster than the latest propeller-driven fighters, but I felt its manoeuvrability was so limited by heavy control forces as to make it useless in combat.

By the time I had reached 485mph it was almost out of fuel and I had to head back, hopefully in time to land at Manston.

The Meteors were singularly unsuccessful against the V1 attack that summer and despite repeated exaggerated claims over the years they only managed to destroy nine confirmed V1s in the time when the neighbouring Tempests had shot down 638.

Later in 1946 I took part in development testing at Gloster's on the Meteor 4 development and this was also a disappointment. With Derwent V engines the RAF had set up an official world speed record with a Mk 4 at over 600mph in the previous year, and planned to raise this again in 1946.

It was my task to clear the two special aircraft to a safe margin above the speed aimed for in the new record.

This was done with some excitement when we encountered 'compressibility' pitch-down rather dangerously at the absolute maximum the Meteor was capable of at about 100ft over the sea, but that was all. The Meteor was still a heavy, cumbersome aircraft with poor manoeuvrability at low and medium altitude and

The author flying the Canberra B2 prototype, VX165, photographed over the Pennines by Charles Sims (no zoom lens) in 1950.

virtually none at all for practical purposes above 40,000ft.

When the Canberra was tested in direct comparison with the latest Meteor VIII at Boscombe Down in 1949 they found on the climb that the Meteor was still at 35,000ft when the Canberra had reached 40,000ft; that the Meteor spun out when they tried to out-turn the Canberra at 30,000ft, and that the Meteor could only reach Mach 0.73 in level flight at 40,000ft where the Canberra was doing 0.81! The Canberra also had a 10,000ft higher manoeuvre ceiling than the Meteor.

So the Meteor did not feature in my favourite aeroplane category, but the brilliant Canberra did. It was described in detail in Chapter 3 and has remained for all time as one of my favourites!

In a memorable visit to California in 1948 my one flight in the second prototype North American XP86, forerunner of the famous Sabre, was an inspiring glimpse into the near future. Here for the first time was a genuine transonic aeroplane with immediately recognisable qualities of a fine fighter.

I enjoyed that aeroplane from the start and it would undoubtedly have become a favourite if I had not been limited to only one flight!

Then the P1. English Electric's supersonic technology demonstrator for the coming Mach 2 Lightning fighter for the RAF was on preparation for First Flight in August 1954, and it was the subject of much contention about the viability of its radical sixty-degree wing-sweep and low-tailplane configuration which had been much criticised by RAE Farnborough.

But I had great confidence in Warton's design team after five years of success with Canberras and particularly in Ray Creasey's aerodynamics department, so on the day I was looking forward to an interesting flight in a new field – no-one had ever flown a sixty-degree swept-wing fighter before, and this was in the days well before 'Virtual Reality' simulation in which to prior-train the pilot!

It was almost a non-event! WG760 responded to the new irreversible hydraulic power-controls smoothly, and took off at the predicted speed exactly as planned.

Its handling in the first scheduled 'flight envelope' to 450KIAS at 15,000ft was simplicity itself, and with some adverse weather approaching I turned back for Boscombe.

Slowing down to check wheels and flaps down was entirely innocuous. Trims and control responses were all comfortable, and I called Boscombe Tower for a practice approach. All systems were in order.

This was the first time in this entirely new and potentially the first British truly supersonic aircraft, and yet I felt increasingly comfortable with it and as if I had flown it many times already.

On turning finals for Boscombe's main runway it had started to rain and I noted that vision through the front flat windscreen panel was reducing, but not so through the curved side 'quarter panels'.

Now on final approach, controllability was so good that it might have been a well-tried straight-wing fighter but I reminded myself about the anticipated high induced-drag of this wing and refrained, as briefed, from reducing power until reaching the runway.

Speed stability and overall control had been so good that I called the Tower and said 'This will be for landing' as we crossed the threshold at about 160kt and flared smoothly, throttling back and touching down gently nose-high as if the P1 had been doing this for years.

Streaming the drag 'chute killed the roll-out speed quickly. The brakes were hardly needed on Boscombe's 10,000ft runway, and Britain's supersonic research programme had begun.

In the next two years of exploring the full capabilities of WG760 we eventually reached Mach 1.5. No major problems occurred and a number of significant discoveries were made leading to valuable changes for the Lightning, which was due to fly in 1957.

During all this work it was soon apparent that the P1, far from being a potentially critical and 'high risk' aeroplane, was in fact smooth, undemanding and delightful to fly with the additional bonus of high excess power from its twin Sapphire engines which provided excellent single-engine safety, always encouraging to have in experimental flying.

It also slid through Mach 1 on its third flight with none of the bucketing about in transonic compressibility that occurred in all the previous generation of fighters.

The P1 was a real pilot's aeroplane and our test-pilots queued to fly it. It received similar accolades at Boscombe Down, and in those pioneering years 1954–56 the P1 was certainly my favourite aeroplane!

It also set the standard which the pilots called for in the flying controls of the Lightning itself; and although this was enthusiastically supported by Aerodynamics, there were some grumbles along the way in the design office before these same brilliant handling qualities were achieved over the whole flight envelope in the RAF's first Mach 2 fighter.

The first flight of the P1B/Lightning prototype XA847 which took place on 4 April 1957 was certainly an exhilarating occasion.

Although a largely different aircraft, the basic configuration was that proved on the P1 but with new engines, systems and cockpit it had more than twice the power.

These were only the major changes of significance to the first flight and I was looking forward to an interesting experience – it proved to be more than that!

With a take-off weight of about 29,000lb, the two reheat Avon engines gave over 30,000lb of thrust – a positive power-to-weight ratio which could theoretically allow the aircraft to climb vertically from take-off. And this is what the RAF did with them later in their historic first showing at the Farnborough Air Show.

The first flight would be more decorous however, but as it had been agreed that engine power should not be reduced (in this new installation) initially until reaching a 'safe' height, I had realised that to keep the speed down at full 'dry thrust' until the undercarriage was fully retracted would involve a climb-out at about forty-five degrees.

It certainly must have looked spectacular to the onlookers, some of whom complained afterwards that the new prototype had been put at risk by an 'aerobatic take-off'! But in the cockpit all was straightforward, if at a rather steep angle.

XA847 rotated smoothly and continued in its breathtaking climb with handling that could not be distinguished from the P1 in this phase.

It was all so satisfactory that after retracting the undercarriage I continued the exhilarating 'Max. Dry' climb, checking engines and systems continuously until after about three and a half minutes I levelled out at 30,000ft and, before trimming out, with only the slightest tremor the Machmeter jumped to 1.02 – supersonic in 'Dry' thrust!

Handling here was indistinguishable from the P1 and I finally reduced power with M 1.2 showing, still without reheat.

In handling and systems checks at a rather more leisurely rate in the descent back to base it became apparent that here was another brilliant prototype.

There were technical problems and some critical incidents on the way, but the clearance in the next two years of the Lightning to Mach 2 plus and ceiling over 70,000ft revealed a fighter of altogether exceptional handling qualities which became widely known as the most manoeuvrable Mach 2 all-weather interceptor of its generation.

The author flying the second development prototype P1B/Lightning at Warton in 1957.

Severe engineering problems and initial underestimation of the scale of support needed in the 1960s caused the authorities to plan for its early retirement, but in the event the Lightning remained in acclaimed operational service for twenty-seven years until its retirement in 1988 when the Binbrook Wing pilots were still saying that they 'could see off anything they met in the skies of Europe'!

In all those development years when my colleagues and I in Warton Flight Operations were able to help the engineers (sometimes with some arguments!) to fine-tune the Lightning's handling qualities to the finest in its class in the world, the Lightning was indeed my favourite aircraft!

There was an interesting interlude in 1963. The great BAC, VC10 four-engined airliner was in initial testing at Vickers' test airfield at Wisley in the hands of Jock Bryce.

I joined him for a fuel consumption and performance test sortie on 6 May 1963.

It was a fine early-summer evening and this great aircraft climbed smoothly through a stratocumulus layer towards the West Country. It was impressively vibrationless and quiet on the flight deck and there was no noticeable disturbance as we climbed through broken cloud into the endless visibility above.

The flight deck was calm and the R/T quiet with little apparently going on. The aircraft was not on autopilot, but the pilot's control movements were small and sometimes almost imperceptible.

At 40,000ft over Cornwall and with the Scilly Islands in sight ahead the Machmeter read an impressive Mach 0.9.

After two four-minute levels at varying power Bryce moved into the right seat and gave me his. Next was a full power level at 41,000ft. This gave Mach 0.91 and I felt that there was a gentle phugoid about the altimeter reading I was trying to hold. Bryce said this was under investigation and was not apparent at lower levels.

The sun was now slipping beyond the horizon and it was becoming dark below. 'Back home' said Bryce, and I eased this fine aeroplane smoothly round onto reciprocal from about twenty miles west of the Scillies, and set it into a gentle descent at M 0.70 with power reduced to close to idling.

Hand-flying this aeroplane was simple, and it had the responses of a Canberra though with increased lateral stability.

It was a delightful, almost restful sensation drifting down across Cornwall, Somerset, Hampshire towards Surrey in the gathering dusk.

Nothing seemed to be happening except that the control responses of this fine aeroplane were satisfying in the relaxed ambience of this spacious flight deck.

With the lights of Guildford in sight to starboard I steered the VC10 gently towards the downwind leg for a westerly approach to Wisley whose runway lights were now clear in the near-darkness.

I wondered when Bryce would want to take over but then he said, 'Join base leg – I'll give you the numbers,' and with his engine speeds and u/c and flap speeds I rolled this large uncomplicated aircraft smoothly onto finals on the now

The author flying the first Argentinian Canberra B Mk62 on the 20th anniversary of the type's first flight at Warton on 13 May 1969. *(BAe Systems)*

One of the first Argentinian Canberra B Mk62s in final finish for delivery in June 1969. *(BAe Systems)*

Flying at Warton for the 30th anniversary of the Canberra's first flight. The author (right) with W/Cdr Harcourt. *(BAe Systems)*

The author with the RAF's most experienced Canberra pilot, S/Ldr Watson (right) and (left) F/O Baker, at the opening of the 40th Canberra celebration at Wyton in 1989. *(Author)*

The 40th anniversary. The Canberra has just landed at Wyton with the author aboard in 1989. *(Author)*

Celebrating forty years of the Canberra at Wyton. *(Author)*

An RAF Canberra T4 painted in the colours of the first prototype VN799 flying from Warton on the 50th anniversary of the type on 13 May 1999. *(BAe Systems)*

A Canberra PR9, still in service with the RAF seen taking off at Warton in 1999. *(BAe Systems)*

The author, Chief Test Pilot of The English Electric Company, in the cockpit of the prototype P1, WG760, at Warton in 1954. *(BAe Systems)*

The author flying the second prototype P1B Lightning, XA853, on test from Warton in 1957. *(BAe Systems)*

One of the
first Lightning
T54s for Saudi
Arabia at
Warton before
delivery in
1966.
(BAe Systems)

A Lightning Mk6 of the Binbrook Wing in the 1970s.

Lightnings Mk1A (nearest), MkT4 and MkT5. *(Author)*

The TSR2 on test from Warton in February 1965. *(BAe Systems)*

Air brake tests being flown by Jimmy Dell in the TSR2 in February 1965. *(BAe Systems)*

The Warton Air Force in 1978. In ascending order; Panavia Tornado, SEPECAT Jaguar, Strikemaster, Lightning Mk6 and Canberra. *(BAe Systems)*

quite dark approach with the approach lights gleaming ahead.

This was all remarkable. I had never landed this brand-new prototype in day-light before and now I was landing it on a flare-path in the dark!

But it came down smoothly, still reminding me of a slightly heavier Canberra, in the centre of the visual approach slope indicators and over the runway thresh-old at about 50ft, Bryce said 'Flare and power off.'

I did this and the great aircraft responded precisely. There was a rumble from behind and a voice from the back said, 'Our end's down Skip. How about yours'!

On the centre-line between the runway lights I eased the wheel forward to lower the nosewheel into contact. Bryce engaged the thrust reversers, and then we turned gently to back-track and do another circuit before taxying off to the main hangars.

I had completed my first landings in a jet airliner, and in darkness!

This was a remarkable demonstration of the simplicity and quality of the VC10, and of the confidence of Jock Bryce in the very early days of this fine aeroplane.

Had I had the opportunity of a few more flights in this exceptional aeroplane I have no doubt that it would have become my favourite heavy jet! It did howev-er become my favourite for passenger travel for many years to come.

In 1964 what became a major sensation in British Aviation began to emerge in the shape of the TSR2 taxying tests at Boscombe Down.

The chaotic gestation period of this strike/reconnaissance aircraft on which the future of the RAF in the decades of the 70s, 80s and 90s and beyond was based, has been well chronicled and will doubtless be quoted for all time as a clas-sic example of how not to procure a new aircraft.

Nevertheless out of this Whitehall farce and industrial confusion some brilliant engineers and administrators produced a prototype in 1964 that finally began tri-als at the 'neutral testing airfield' which had been specified mysteriously by the Vickers Company – Boscombe Down.

Taxying trials were completed by the end of September and with Don Bowen, flight test observer, in the back seat, I flew XR219 for the first time on 27 September.

The flight met all scheduled test points and produced only one major techni-cal problem. This was with the undercarriage and would need investigation.

But one very positive aspect emerged. From take-off onwards throughout the flight I could not fault the control and stability in any aspect.

After take-off three-axis responses had been so good that I had just got on with the scheduled observations, and some of my own, without the need for further cautious exploration of actual flying qualities. This untried prototype might just as well have been an already developed and proved aeroplane!

After one lengthy circuit of Boscombe I decided to continue a second as pro-visionally planned, and at this stage to make sure that I had not missed something I investigated stick and rudder pulses again more thoroughly in pitch, roll and yaw. This was surprising and satisfying!

The aeroplane felt 'geared to the stick' on all axes, and the response rates and 'feel' were ideal for these circuit conditions.

The undercarriage had not been cleared for retraction on this flight, limiting our speed to no more than 275KIAS where there was mild but not excessive buffet; and then the slow-down to assess approach handling in the landing configuration.

At 180kt and with no change in the mild buffet which I now identified as from the thirty-degree 'blown' flap in use, there was no change at all in control responses. I could not sense any noise or controllability changes between 275 and 175KIAS. Co-ordinating heading and height was merely a case of 'steering the gauges'.

It was weird. This was like flying the Warton simulator, but easier!

This precise controllability was apparent right down to the landing, and again I noted the precision of heading-holding and approach-slope holding, and of speed stability on the approach.

Still with this 'geared to the stick' feeling of the elevator the flare to a low-rate touchdown was so straightforward that the next thing was a sharp surprise! As the main wheels touched a very violent oscillation occurred at the cockpit, so severe that it momentarily blurred my vision. But this cleared as I throttled back and the speed dropped and then, still nose-high at about 140KIAS I streamed the drag 'chute and this fascinating first-flight came to an end.

The undercarriage-induced airframe oscillation was with us for the rest of the test programme, but at the time of the subsequent cancellation a modification with 'damper' struts was well on the way to curing this condition which had resulted from the effects of 'spin-up'-drag setting off the fuselage natural frequency via the main undercarriage oleos.

In the rest of the short test programme the flight envelope was explored to 500KIAS at very low level and to 600KIAS a little higher; and also slow-speed handling down to landings at 150KIAS. At supersonic speed at 30,000ft and at 500KIAS through the valleys of the Pennines down to 50ft above the hillsides the prototype showed this unusually high degree of precise, undisturbed controllability.

Even as early as Flight 1 I had written in my flight report, 'in this configuration and under these test conditions TSR2 could be flown safely by any pilot qualified on Lightning or similar aircraft.'

Apart from some very minor adjustments to lateral control gearing, nearly 50% of the performance envelope of this fast and heavy aircraft had already been cleared as very satisfactory with no need for modification.

It felt as though it was flying on auto-pilot (none fitted on the prototype) and that there seemed to be no limit to its potential – though the design limits had of course yet to be proved.

Jimmy Dell said of it after his first TSR2 flight, 'It's a pilot's aeroplane all the way.'

At the point of cancellation after only twenty-four flights I had already recommended that the RAF customer should fly it to confirm our findings.

But the politicians ensured that the RAF lost their vital long-range strike and reconnaissance capability for the future, with no replacement in sight.

With its supreme ease of control in all the conditions tested, TSR2 was for me in 1965 my favourite aeroplane!

But after all these fascinating experiences it all comes down to the bottom line. The Canberra and Lightning were the very favourite aeroplanes of my flying life.

Epilogue

ighlights of those forty years and some conclusions. So many lasting memories of events great and small but none more poignant than the Battle of Britain

Today in the year 2001, in the litany of misconception that has been developed about that historic period by historians and media men with escalating enthusiasm and too often with little restraint in terms of accuracy, responsibility or good taste, it must be difficult if not impossible for the new generations to obtain a true feeling for or understanding of that fight for the very survival of this nation.

By the end of June 1940 the country had effectively lost an army and its protective air force in defeat in France. By miraculous organisation and courage the Royal Navy and 'the small ships' had recovered from Dunkirk the majority of our soldiers and some thousands of the French Army, but all their equipment and *matériel* were left behind on the beaches, and over 400 Hurricane fighters had been lost. Heavy losses had indeed been inflicted on the enemy, but not to the extent of blunting the momentum of their victorious drive to the Channel coast. Now, Germany proclaimed, it was to be *'Gegen Engelandt'*.

In this stunned country the population could barely see at first what was inevitably developing but one small group in air force blue uniform, the pilots of Fighter Command of the Royal Air Force, could see what was coming very clearly.

Prime Minister Churchill brilliantly set the scene for the nation, 'We shall fight on the beaches . . . and in the air . . . we shall never surrender.' But the fighter pilots could see with their newly experienced clarity that there would be no fighting on the beaches until the RAF had been defeated over the Channel.

They knew this and the German High Command knew this but dismissed the idea with arrogance, and the RAF could see that they had a job to do.

The commanding officer of one Hurricane squadron (*see* Appendix 1) talking to his pilots, many of them now 'veterans' of the battle over France, said:

> 'No-one is going to stop the Huns invading this country in the next month or so except us. When we have cleared the bastards out of the skies of the Channel and the south coast they won't be able to invade by sea.
>
> 'So we are going to stop them. There's nobody else and we are in a proud position and the luckiest people in the country at this time. This is what we are here for, so now lets get on with it!'

The summer months of 1940 soon brought increasing armadas of hundreds of German bombers and fighters across the Channel to attack our fighter stations, radar posts, and finally in desperation when these measures had failed to eliminate Fighter Command, in September came the mass attacks on the capital itself, London.

The battles which ranged along the South Coast, over Dorset, Sussex, Kent and Greater London have been chronicled, exaggerated, distorted and sometimes even derided in the timeless way of the media to such an extent that much of the quality of those times is in danger of being lost to sight.

Television has perhaps been most culpable in the their determination that the public should see the battle through their eyes – that is the eyes of a generation of producers and presenters who were not born at the time, determined to see every aspect through the perspectives of the year 2001.

In their frequent total concentration on the 'horrors of battle', and on 'post-traumatic-stress-disorder' and 'counselling' (which had not even been invented in 1940) they have comprehensively failed to identify and project the core feelings and emotions of that time in the Fighter squadrons.

With a very few exceptions the atmosphere and morale in the squadrons was exactly what the RAF had planned.

'This is what we are here for and have been training for. We were outnumbered in France but never beaten – we can see off the Krauts and now let's do it,' was the spirit in the squadrons.

There was no misery 'at Readiness' in the squadron 'Dispersals', but much joking and laughter – nervous possibly but always that aspect was controlled and dismissed. You were never going to let your friends down and to see the funny side, and there was much that was hilarious.

Then after the fighting and the excited debriefing with the Intelligence Officer – just a statement of what you did and saw and no hysterical claims of 'victories', the theme so loved by the media of today. Then the real enjoyment at the end of the day with a few beers before finding somewhere to eat, then a few hours' sleep before going back to the airfield for the next day's Dawn Readiness to face it all again. No thoughts for the future; there was no point in that.

For 18–25 year olds it was all an immense adrenalin rush. Flying the world's best fighters was wonderful. We were the only people still fighting the enemy in the air and we were defending our own homeland and folk with everything at stake, often even over our own home towns and villages.

The media in 2001 made relentless efforts to project the idea of low morale in the squadrons in face of heavy casualties, and of course in a few cases where losses became so high that a squadron had to be withdrawn from the battle to re-equip and retrain, there were cases of stress. But contrary to the media's black-and-white ideas of 'courage' and 'cowardice', all fighting men have fears that they learn to control. This is a vital part of their professionalism and becomes easier to control with experience and survival.

Nevertheless there are inevitably a very few people who are unable to withstand the strains of combat, and in recent times the media have identified with enthusiasm some of those who suffered, for entirely understandable reasons, in the Battle of Britain and who now after sixty years have been persuaded to talk about it in terms that imply blame on others with absolutely no justification. In fact, overall one of the most striking and significant features of the battles for Britain in 1940 was the resilient, laughing and loyal dedication of all those on the ground and in the air who fought that battle.

It had its terrors and many moments of sadness, but most survivors remember it as the finest time of their lives. We were saving our country and we were winning.

That spirit may be summarised by quoting one young squadron commander in August who, when leading his formation of eight Hurricanes headlong into a mass bomber attack reported as '120 plus heading for Portland,' then called over the radio, 'Targets ahead. Come on chaps let's surround them!'

Then, after the defeat of the enemy over England in 1940 the RAF fighters took to the offensive from 1941, and in 1943 the development and initial successes of the Hawker Typhoon heavy fighters led ultimately in 1944 to their major victories at Mortain and Falaise in the battle of Normandy and on through to the final battles for Germany in 1945. These were unforgettable experiences, as were leading the new Hawker Tempests in 1944 over the Normandy invasion beaches. Then against the enemy's last massive attack on the South of England and London by the V1 flying bombs, and finally on into Belgium and the victorious battles for Germany, by now not with just one squadron but with five squadrons of the RAF's tremendous fighter pilots whose sheer courage, humour, pride and loyalty were such a warm privilege to share and a never to be forgotten experience.

After the ceasefire came the fascinating investigations into the problems of transonic flight which had begun for me in 1942 and now reached the threshold of supersonics in 1948.

One's first supersonic dive in that year in America; then the first British fully-supersonic prototype in 1954 and reaching Mach 2 in its successor in 1958 and finally reaching supersonic speed in the first British supersonic bomber in 1965, were all unique and memorable occasions, as indeed was flying the Atlantic twice in one day with my comrades in 1952 (the first time ever).

Defining moments were of course rejecting the chance in 1946 of a permanent commission and a peacetime career in the Service I loved, the RAF; and in 1964 declining the offer to be chief test pilot for the Concorde supersonic airliner programme.

Neither of these decisions was easy, and they were the subject of much heart-searching and debate with my so-strong-right-arm Pat who would I think have preferred the RAF option, but not the Concorde. She succeeded however in letting me feel that my preferences were hers also.

In July 1979 my last main task in the aviation industry was completed with the delivery of the first international Tornado to NATO; a successful design which put the British, German and Italian air forces right at the cutting edge of world military technology and was soon to become a major success weapon for the Allied Forces in the Gulf war.

All these years had been momentous and inspirational. A most wonderful marriage and family and my own miraculous survival to enjoy them. The inspiring friendships of the fighter pilots, and the warm professional associations with the test pilots, engineers and all those in our joint endeavours in pioneering the jet and supersonic era in Britain's centre of military aviation design in the North West.

None of the fighter pilots had expected to survive 1940 and sadly many did not, but few of the survivors would have expected to see the year 2000 – I would be eighty and I achieved this on 10 August, but sadly without my dear wife Pat who died with extraordinary bravery in 1999.

Now, sixty-one years on from 1940, those of us still here look around at what is left of the England we knew. There is precious little.

Our world has advanced with the technology explosion in an unprecedented rush of materialism, with our population said to be enjoying a vast increase in wealth, housing and possessions. Car usage has increased to the point where every car is competing for just one car space in every city, town and motorway in the country. Car journey times can now take twice as long as they did only twenty years ago, and trains no longer run on time.

The beauty of the countryside in the United Kingdom (if that title is still valid) appears from the air to be unchanged, but in many counties a close look reveals vast areas of once pure rivers and streams now running polluted beyond recognition and in so many cases now devoid of the wonderful runs of migrating salmon and sea-trout that filled them in the past.

In the monoculture farmlands throughout the land the natural balance of nature has been damaged, and in many areas destroyed, by the avalanche of chemical spraying which has persisted for fifty years for the sole purpose of profit; and has resulted in dramatic reduction of the small bird, mammal and insect populations and even in the disappearance of some species with many others at risk.

The deafening dawn-chorus of the 1930s and the continuous song of skylarks all over the sheeplands of the South are just memories today. Where can a nightingale be heard? There was one near almost every garden in the South only fifty years ago.

These are only a few examples of the dramatic decline in our natural heritage which we have all thoughtlessly allowed to happen in the lemming-rush to recover prosperity after a long and terrible war.

But in doing this we have not banished poverty in our own country, nor have we resolved desperate problems in the management of healthcare, housing, education and the upbringing of our future generations, or the grinding steadily to a halt of our national transport system.

In my life I have been so fortunate in always having the freedom of the skies to escape to from this gloomy awareness of what is happening all around us, and often after soaring at 40,000ft in a glorious golden sunset I have slanted down through rose-pink cloud valleys to curve in towards the home-base runway lights gleaming in the gathering dusk to settle my fighter into the final approach, passing over endless lines of headlights streaming below as they head homewards in the rush hour.

Then after stopping engines and completing the formalities of the day I have driven my car to join the chaos outside the gates, there to be engulfed by the tension, road rage and sheer angst of the commuters trying to get home to TV and whatever else awaits them.

But it has all been a great experience, often joyful and always challenging; and now I can no longer escape above the clouds to the visibility that goes on forever and have rejoined the rest of the less fortunate human race, I look back with immense gratitude for all those years in aviation in which, with my splendid colleagues, I strived, achieving with all due humility more successes than failures, to help in a very small way to put this country into the forefront of world aviation.

It was, I am afraid, a rather selfish life made possible only by the never-ending support of my wonderful wife and family.

But how I would love to do it all over again.

R.P.B. November 2000

APPENDIX 1

The Battle of Britain 1940

This brief summary by an RAF administrative officer at the time, remains profoundly relevant sixty years on. John Strachey (distinguished politician in post-war Britain) was adjutant of 87 Squadron and when the CO, Squadron Leader 'Widge' Gleed, published his book *Arise to Conquer* (Victor Gollancz), Strachey's foreword was and still is in 2001, outstanding:

'It is already clear that the Battle of Britain must ever remain one of decisive engagements in world history. However long this second world war lasts, however gigantic, portentous and overwhelming its developments may be, the series of air engagements which took place over the eastern and southern parts of Britain between July and November 1940 must remain its first turning point. They played, in much more desperate circumstances, the same rôle as was played by the Battle of the Marne in the first world war. The repulse of the air attack on Britain did not mean (by how many years, how many million deaths, how many prodigious events, we do not yet know) that the Fascist attempt to conquer the world had failed. On the contrary, the point at issue was that that attempt must have succeeded if the Battle of Britain had been lost.

If the tiny number of British fighter squadrons which were at that time airworthy had then been overborne, none of the rest of the gathering of forces which will at last be adequate to the defeat of Nazi Germany and her Allies; neither the subsequent British recovery; nor the Russian resistance; nor the American entry into the war, could have taken place. The disproportion between the illimitable stake and the minute force involved is breathtaking.

I cannot but suppose that both the contemporary reader and the future historian will turn to this book when they wish to know what the pilots who did this thing were like. For it seems to me that once they have read it they will know. They are here depicted with an artlessness which the most experienced authors will profoundly envy; "Watty", eternally making his model aeroplanes in the dispersal huts; the resilient, the irrepressible "Rubber", "Roddy" with his affectation of extreme disinterest in the war and his off-hand charm; and the author himself whom the reader will get to know best of all.

These, and just a few hundred more, were the pilots who did it. It was they who, when the telephone rang in dispersal – when Ops said, "One hundred plus; or a hundred and fifty plus; or two hundred plus; are crossing the coast," jumped into their cockpits, took off and fought the enemy.

In doing so, they settled the kind of lives which all of us, and our children, and probably their children, will lead.

We are bound to feel an insatiable curiosity as to what they were like, how they felt while they were fighting, and why they did it.

The simplest, and in my view the most exciting, thing which emerges is the fact that they felt frightened. That, if you come to think of it, is their ultimate claim to glory. If they had been Nazi or Japanese robots, mentally conditioned by some

process of mass intoxication, some loathsome but effective scheme of mental muti-
lation, by which they had been dehumanised, hypnotised into actually liking death
and destruction for the sake of some Führer, then the whole thing would have been
incomparably less remarkable, and incomparably less worthwhile. But in fact as the
reader will see they were, and are, just young Englishmen with the same likes, dis-
likes, hopes, fears and expectations as the rest of their generation. They were, and
are, profoundly capable of the normal, constructive pursuits of peaceful existence;
they are not one jot dehumanised or brutalised; they remain intensely individual,
intensely themselves; and, nevertheless, they were able to do what they did.'

*'Watty' Watson, Harry Tait, 'Widge' Gleed, 'Roddy' Rayner and Peter Comely of No. 87 Squadron taken
in 1940.*

'Watty' Watson with Hurricane 1 of No. 87 Squadron in 1940.

Cowley, 'Rubber' Thoroughgood and 'Roddy' Rayner.

APPENDIX 2

From the archives of 609 (WR) Squadron Association:

Date. 24/12/42

Squadron Routine Orders
By
Squadron Leader R. P. Beamont. DFC
Commanding
No. 609 (West Riding) Squadron. Royal Air Force Station. Manston
SPECIAL ORDERS OF THE DAY.

The following message was addressed to me personally from the A.O.C. in C; 21 December 1942

'I wish to congratulate you, and 609 Squadron, on the very excellent results you have been obtaining recently.

I am very much impressed with your own night "Intruder" operations, and I thought that the performance put up by Flight Lieutenant De Selys, and Sergeant Turek yesterday was quite first class.

I would like you to convey my congratulations to all your pilots on their excellent work.

With all good wishes to the Squadron for 1943.'

(Signed)   T. Leigh-Mallory.

The following was received from AOC No. 11 Group.

'I am extremely pleased to see that your Unit managed to knock down some of the tip and run Fw.190s during the last day or two.

It is very gratifying to see that the Typhoon is at last coming into its own. Please convey my congratulations to all concerned.'

(Signed) H. Saunders.

I wish to extend my thanks to all ranks who, by their constant labour have contributed so greatly to these results.

(Signed) R. P. Beamont

Squadron Leader, Commanding, No. 609 (WR) Squadron

Appendix 2A

An Early Brush with the Press

There are Lies, Dammed Lies, and Reporters 'Bull'. An example from 609 Squadron Association Archives.

Reference: DE/RPB

No. 609 (WR) Squadron
Royal Air Force Station
Manston, Kent
6 March 1943

Squadron Leader Tomlinson
Public Relations
No. 11 Group

Dear Squadron Leader Tomlinson,

As you know representatives of the Press visited this unit on Thursday 4 March, with a view to obtaining material for a story about the measures taken to combat tip and run raiders.

The results of this appeared in the Press today, 6 March 1943. In the Times, Telegraph, Mirror, Mail and Sketch, the situation was described reasonably accurately and very fairly. The last three papers quoted me word for word in such a way as to give a fair impression of the Typhoon's work and what we think of it.

I wish however to lodge the strongest possible protest against the publishing, in the Daily Express, of an article entitled 'Achtung Typhoon' by Basil Cardew.

Mr Cardew has so far allowed his imagination to run riot as to describe and even quote, in some 500 words, a purely fictitious conversation with me.

I did in fact have some two minutes conversation with the gentleman, and the substance of this was exactly the same as that quoted by other correspondents At <u>no</u> time was there any reference to 'Ghost' men or 'Achtung Typhoon' etc! Such statements as these can only be regarded as laughable by the services and the knowledgeable public, and this squadron feels that the publication of such insidious bilge is not only harmful to its reputation, but is also a very poor return for the trouble taken to entertain the Press during a normal hard working day of operations.

Yours sincerely

R. P. Beamont
Squadron Leader, Commanding 609 (WR) Squadron

P.S. During my 22 years I have been called many things, but never Bob!

The article in question.

Daily Express. Saturday 6 March 1943

'Achtung Typhoon', they cry now

'Ghost' men beat sneak raiders

By Basil Cardew

RAF Fighter Station. S.E. Coast, Friday

After a three point landing, Bob Beamont taxied his Typhoon fighter across the airfield, switched off his 2,000 horsepower engine, vaulted from the cockpit and came towards me with one of the largest grins I have seen in years. 'Shake hands with a ghost man,' he laughed, 'for we are the ghost men of the RAF'.

APPENDIX 3

Letter from Lord Balfour, Secretary of State for Air

Air Ministry
King Charles Street
Whitehall W1
8 February 1943

Dear Beamont,

I must send you this line to tell you with what wonder and admiration all of us watched your take-off and flying of the Typhoon yesterday, when you left for Manston. Not only did it impress those like myself, who have not got the knowledge of others, but I wish you could have heard the comments of the Spitfire experts. They said they did not realise the Typhoon could be handled like that.

It was a great pleasure to meet you and have an opportunity of saying how much I admire the particular work on which you and your Squadron are engaged.

I look forward to seeing you at Manston in the not too distant future.

Squadron Leader R. P. Beamont, DFC
   Royal Air Force Station
      Manston
         Kent

Yours sincerely,
Harold Balfour

Letter from AVM Hugh Saunders, Air Officer Commanding No. 11 Group Fighter Command

<u>PERSONAL</u>

Headquarters, No. 11 Group
Royal Air Force
UXBRIDGE
Middlesex

<u>DO/HWLS</u>

14 May 1943

Dear *Beamont*

I should like to congratulate you on your very well deserved DSO. Your work with No. 609 Squadron was outstanding and has done much to develop Typhoon technique.

I hope you will have an enjoyable rest with Hawkers, and I look forward to your return to No. 11 Group in due course.

Yours *sincerely*
H Saunders

Squadron Leader R. P. Beamont, DSO, DFC
   Whin Cottage
      Sandheath Road
         HINDHEAD
            Surrey

Appendix 4

Letter from Air Marshal Sir Trafford Leigh-Mallory, C-in-C Fighter Command

TLM/30   21 May 1943

Dear *Beaumont*

My very hearty congratulations to you on being awarded a very well earned DSO.
2. No. 609 Squadron has had a most successful career under your leadership, and I attribute their success very largely to your own personal efforts.
3. Good luck to you in the future!

Yours *very truly*
Trafford · Leigh-Mallory

Squadron Leader R. P. Beamont, DSO, DFC
No. 609 Squadron
RAF Station
<u>MANSTON</u>

Letter from Lord Balfour

Air Ministry
King Charles Street
Whitehall W1

Dear *Beamont*   24 May 1943

I send you this line of most hearty congratulations on your DSO. Directly I saw you, your Squadron, the Typhoons and the work they were doing, I knew that it was inevitable.

I do hope your face is none the worse for meeting the instrument panel, because the last I heard of you you were in Deal hospital.

I hope to come and see your Unit as soon as possible.

Yours sincerely,
Harold Balfour

Squadron Leader R. P. Beamont, DFC, DSO
Royal Air Force Station
HQ No. 11 Group
Uxbridge, Middlesex

Appendix 5

The *Daily Sketch* Monday 24 May 1943

'Master of Typhoon' wins DSO

Squadron-Leader R. P. Beamont, DFC, has put 25 locomotives and many lorries out of action. He is known in the RAF as 'the master pilot of the Typhoons'.

Now this 'outstanding leader' has been awarded the DSO.

He was lent to the Hawker Aircraft Company when the Typhoon was being developed, and is now in command of the West Riding Squadron which has destroyed many 'sneak' raiders and shot up more than 100 locomotives.

Appendix 6

London *Evening Standard*. 21 June 1944

Big Percentage of Fly Bombs Killed

From JAMES STUART, Evening Standard Air Reporter
A KENTISH FIGHTER STATION, Wednesday

The man chiefly responsible for beating the Nazis' flying-bomb in the daytime is 25-year-old Wing Commander R. P. Beamont, DSO, DFC and Bar.

'Bob', boyish-looking fighter ace and test pilot, commands a station from which the Tempest, Britain's latest fighter airplane and the fastest in the world, is helping to take much of the sting out of Hitler's no-longer-secret weapon.

Since the enemy launched the winged bomb attacks last Thursday, Beamont's station has provided the most successful counter.

APPENDIX 7

NWH V BIG GPK 1/30 OP
T NEWCHURCH

[TELEX] FROM A.O.C. NO. 11 GROUP
TO NEWCHURCH FOR W/CDR BEAMONT
INFO ADGB BIGGIN HILL
QQX BT

A206 29 JUNE
PLEASE ACCEPT FOR YOURSELF AND CONVEY TO OFFICERS COM-
MANDING NOS. 3, 486 AND 56 SQUADRONS AND ALL PILOTS OF THE
NEWCHURCH WING THE HEARTIEST CONGRATULATIONS OF ALL
MEMBERS OF MY STAFF AND MYSELF UPON THE DESTRUCTION BY
THEM OF THEIR 200TH PILOTLESS AIRCRAFT. SPECIAL CONGRATU-
LATIONS ALSO TO NO. 3 SQUADRON ON GETTING THEIR FIRST
HUNDRED BY THEMSELVES. WE FOLLOW EACH DAY WITH ADMIRA-
TION THE TRULY SPLENDID WORK YOU ARE DOING WITH SUCH
SKILL AND UNTIRING DETERMINATION

———BOUCHIER———

BT2355B
IS AR K

Appendix 7A

The *Daily Mail*, Tuesday, 25 July 1944

BEAMONT – 1st FLY – BOMB ACE
Wins Fourth Medal
By Daily Mail Reporter

Britain's first ace flying-bomb killer has won another award, it is announced to-day.

He is Acting Wing Commander Roland Prosper Beamont, and he wins a Bar to his DSO. He also holds the DFC and Bar.

Although the citation makes no mention of his successes against flying bombs, it is known that Wing Commander Beamont, in recent weeks, has shot many of the bombs down into the sea.

Appendix 8

From: Air Commodore C. A. Bouchier, CBE, DFC

HEADQUARTERS NO. 11 GROUP
ROYAL AIR FORCE
Reference: UXBRIDGE
CAB/DO   9 September 1944

Dear Beamont

Air Marshal Sir Roderick Hill, KCB, MC, AFC, has received a letter from Sir Ernest Gowers, KC3, KBE, London Regional Defence Commissioner, of which the following is an extract:

> 'At a recent meeting of my Standing Committee of Town Clerks of the London Region a spontaneous and unanimous request was made to me that I should convey to you, on behalf of the Local Authorities in the Region, their deep sense of obligation to the Pilots under your Command whose skill and devotion are doing so much to mitigate London's present ordeal. I gladly do this. We are filled with admiration of their magnificent achievements, and I hope you will find it possible to convey this tribute to them so that they may know how full and gratefully London realises its debt to them.'

I feel the foregoing should be brought to the notice of all Wing Leaders, Squadron Commanders and Pilots concerned, not forgetting the splendid work also done by Control Staffs both at Sector and GCI Stations.

Yours sincerely.

C. Bouchier.

Appendix 8A

Wing Comm. Roland P. Beamont
Distinguished Flying Cross

RESTRICTED

HEADQUARTERS
UNITED STATES AIR FORCES IN EUROPE

APO 633, US Army
GENERAL ORDERS 4 April 1946

NO 87

I. Under the provisions of Army Regulations 600–45, 22 September 1943, as amended, and Circular #28, Hq, US Forces, European Theater, US Army, 6 March 1946, the <u>DISTINGUISHED FLYING CROSS</u> is awarded to the following named Officers:

<u>WING COMMANDER ROLAND PROSPER BEAMONT</u>, DSO, DFC (41819), Central Fighter Establishment, Royal Air Force. For extraordinary achievement in aerial flight against the enemy. During his tours of duty Wing Commander Beamont distinguished himself by outstanding aerial skill and exceptional courage. He was responsible for the development of successful tactics against the flying bombs and destroyed over thirty. His unfailing devotion to duty and determination reflect great credit upon himself and the Royal Air Force.

Appendix 8B

'Ernie' Cross, expert electrical engineer, who had installed the electrical system in the prototype Canberra VN799 in 1949, was a member of the support team at Aldergrove for the 'double-Atlantic' flight in 1952.

He recalled an amusing incident in *The Great Day Dawns*, in which his confident professional knowledge helped to prevent a last-minute cancellation:

'In the dark hours before dawn, Tuesday 26 August 1952 was cool and cloudy, but dry, and Roland Beamont had started the engines and was revving-up and completing cockpit checks prior to take-off.

Then the revs. were cut and a finger pointed at the watching throng. The Deputy Service Manager, Bill Dixon (W.Cdr.(Tech.) Retired), pointed to each of us in turn, and when the finger stopped at me there was a raised thumb from the cockpit – we did not have a ground RT link in those days. Having opened-up and poked my head into the cabin, I was told that the instrument emergency power supply was U/S, and the attempt would have to be scrubbed if it could not be fixed. Bill Dixon was getting tense, and I realised that whatever needed doing would have to be done quickly. The problem was not in deciding where the trouble lay – that was reasonably obvious, the problem was how to attack it. We simply did not have any time in hand.

The Canberra's main equipment compartment is immediately behind the pressure cabin, and contains an enormous electrical junction box that is bolted directly onto the pressure bulkhead. This particular junction box sported a torque switch, which had probably stuck open when Bee cut the main supply, so what to do?

I cannot remember actually reasoning thus, but it must have occurred to me that, as the mechanics had hung up, what was needed was a mechanical shock to get things moving.

I heaved myself into the cabin, walked through to the back and asked Peter Hillwood, in the Bomber's seat, to move over a bit. I then reached up above his head and gave the bulkhead an almighty clout with the side of my clenched fist. The result was both immediate and dramatic: "That's it", called Bee, and he switched back to main supplies, quickly checking the emergency supply switching again, and said that they were off. With all the confidence and impetuosity of youth I agreed that they could go. I wished them luck, dropped out of the cabin, shut the door, and stood back as the aircraft moved off.

At 6.34 a.m., shortly after dawn, and in the faint red light of early morning, they took off for Gander and a date with aviation history. Bill Dixon couldn't believe what I had done, so I told him again, but in the end common sense prevailed. It must have dawned on him that it might not be a good idea to question Roland Beamont's judgement!

An interesting tail piece proves what some of us have always known: as a test pilot, Roland Beamont was incomparable and unique. Some years after the events described above Bee was talking to my father – a noted character in British Aerospace predecessor companies in the period 1938–1963. "I wonder", asked Bee, "if young Ernie ever thought about my feelings when he thumped the electrics back to life and then sent me off across 2,000 miles of water?" "I shouldn't think so", replied my old man. "Well", said Bee, "it occurred to me that if that was all it took, I could get Peter Hillwood to do a bit of thumping if we lost the instrument supplies again". A lesser mortal would simply have abandoned the flight.'

'Ernie' Cross, far right, the expert electrician who had installed the electrical system in the prototype Canberra VN799 in 1949, was a member of the support team at Aldergrove for the 'double-Atlantic' flights in 1952. He recalled an amusing incident in which his confident professional knowledge helped to prevent a last-minute cancellation.

APPENDIX 9

The threshold of the 'Supersonic Era' produced not only a wide range of exotic designs with swept-back wings, but also some significant changes in flight-testing policy from the cautiously progressive to the possibly over-ambitious!

The following list shows that some new designs were actually tested to Mach 1+ during their first ever flights! The list was researched by Al Blackburn, a distinguished test-pilot in the North American Co. in the 1950s, who added, 'I doubt we shall see such crazy antics again!'

Supersonic First Flights in the 1950s

The following aircraft exceeded Mach 1 in level flight on their first flights during the decade of the 1950s:

YF-100A *Super Sabre*, George Welch, North American, 1st Flt. 5/25/53 (George had a second flight the same day and repeated his Mach 1+ performance)

XF-104 *Starfighter*, Tony LeVier, Lockheed, 1st Flt. (w/A/B) 2/28/54 (Tony also was the first to exceed 1000mph on this same flight)

F-101A *VooDoo*, Bob Little, McDonnell Aircraft, 1st Flt. 9/29/54

XF8U-1 *Crusader*, John Konrad, Vought Aircraft, 1st Flt. 5/25/55

YF-105A *Thunderchief*, Rusty Roth, Republic Aircraft, 1st Flt. 11/22/55

F11F-1F *Super Tiger*, Corky Meyer, Grumman Aircraft, 1st Flt. 5/25/56

YF-107A (no name), Bob Baker, North American, 1st Flt. 9/10/56 (Bob had a gear door problem and had to go into a slight dive to exceed Mach 1)

F-106A *Delta Dart*, Dick Johnson, Convair, 1st Flt. 12/26/56 (supersonic on 2nd Flt. 12/27/56)

P1B *Lightning* (prototype), Roland 'Bee' Beamont, English Electric, 1st Flt. 4/4/57, Mach 1.2 (without afterburners)

XF4H *Phantom II*, Bob Little, McDonnell, 1st Flt. 5/27/58 (supersonic on 2nd Flt. 5/28/58)

P11 *Lightning* T Mk 4 Trainer, 'Bee' Beamont, English Electric, 1st Flt. 5/6/59. Mach 1.1

N-156F Freedom Fighter, Lew Nelson, Northrop, 1st Flt. 7/30/59

APPENDIX 10

Warton flight-test plan for Britain's first flight to Mach 2 (twice the speed of sound), carried out successfully on 12 December 1958.

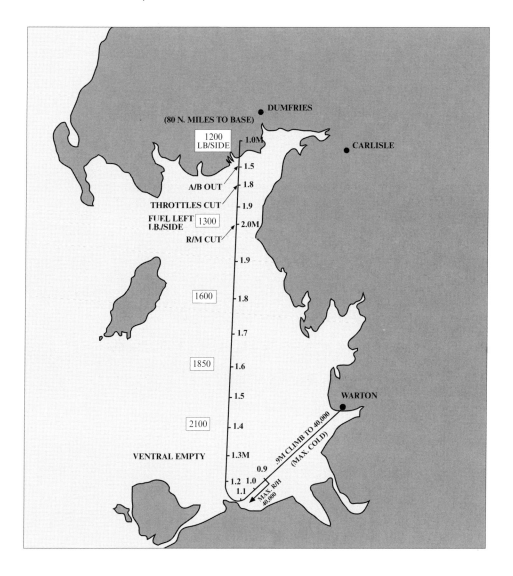

APPENDIX 11

First-time supersonic speeds in a British aircraft.

Date	Aircraft	Altitude (ft)	Speed (Mach)	Place	Pilot
11.8.54	P.1 WG760 *(1st British supersonic level flight)*	30,000	1.02	Boscombe Down	R. P. Beamont
10.10.54	P.1 WG760	30,000	1.13	Warton	R. P. Beamont
3.11.54	P.1 WG760	30,000	1.14	Warton	R. P. Beamont
12.11.54	P.1 WG760	30,000	1.22	Warton	R. P. Beamont
28.2.56	P.1 WG760 (R/H)	33,000	1.45	Warton	R. P. Beamont
28.2.56	P.1 WG760 (R/H)	36,000	1.53	Warton	R. P. Beamont
15.5.57	P.1B Lightning XA847	41,000	1.62	Warton	R. P. Beamont
17.5.57	P.1B Lightning XA847	40,000	1.73	Warton	R. P. Beamont
4.6.57	P.1B Lightning XA847	40,000	1.75	Warton	R. P. Beamont
23.11.57	P.1B Lightning XA847	44,000	1.83	Warton	R. P. Beamont
17.2.58	P.1B Lightning XA856	40,000	1.86	Warton	R. P. Beamont
16.9.58	P.1B Lightning XA847	40,000	1.88	Warton	R. P. Beamont
16.9.58	P.1B Lightning XA847	40,000	1.9	Warton	R. P. Beamont
15.10.58	P.1B Lightning XA847	42,000	1.92	Warton	R. P. Beamont
25.11.58	P.1B Lightning XA847 *(1st British flight to Mach 2)*	40,000	2.00	Warton	R. P. Beamont
3.4.63	Lightning F.2/3 XN734 *(Fastest flight in Lightning)*	39,000	2.105	Warton	R. P. Beamont

'First Flights' by the author, of British prototype aircraft and new type-variants, 1949–1968.

Date	Aircraft type (powerplant)	Serial
1. 13.5.49	B.3/45 Canberra B.1. prototype (RR Avon RA2 engines)	VN799
2. 9.11.49	B.3/45 Canberra B.1 2nd prototype (RR nene engines)	VN828
3. 8.10.50	Canberra B.2 1st production aircraft	WD929
4. 15.7.52	Canberra B.5 modified with RR Avon RA7 engines	VX185
5. 12.6.52	Canberra T.4 trainer prototype	WN467
6. 12.8.52	Canberra PR.3 1st production aircraft	WE135
7. 23.7.54	Canberra B.8 interdictor prototype (converted from B.5)	VX185
8. 4.8.54	P.1 Lightning prototype (AS Sapphire SA5 engines)	WG760
9. 18.7.55	P.1A 2nd prototype with guns and ventral fuel and, later, reheat. Also foot-pedal wheel brakes	WG763
10. 4.4.57	P.1B Lightning, 3rd prototype (RR Avon 24R engines)	XA847
11. 5.9.57	P.1B 5 prototype, engine development aircraft	XA856
12. 3.4.58	P.1B Lightning, 1st pre-production aircraft	XG307
13. 6.5.59	Lightning (P.11) T.4 trainer prototype	XL628
14. 20.9.59	2nd T.4 trainer prototype	XL629
15. 30.11.59	1st production Lightning F.1	XM134
16. 16.8.60	1st production Lightning F.1A	XM169
17. 9.1.62	Lightning F.3 development prototype. New fin	XG310
18. 17.4.64	Lightning F.6 development prototype	XP697
19. 27.9.64	TSR.2 prototype	XR219
20. 24.11.65	Lightning F.6, 1st production aircraft	XR768
21. 29.8.67	Lightning 55 trainer prototype/1st production aircraft	55–711

BIBLIOGRAPHY

Aeronautical Review. A&AEE and RAE reports (1940). Putnam.

Aeroplane Monthly.

Aerospace Heritage. BAe Systems.

Arise to Conquer (1942) Ian Gleed. Victor Gollancz.

Beamont, R. P. Flying Log Books.

Cross, 'Ernie' (1952). *The Great Day Dawns*.

'Intelligence Summary' reports (1944). HQ No. 11 Group, Fighter Command.

Longmate, Norman. *The Doodle Bugs*. Hutchinson.

Report on the introduction of jet airliners (Dec. 1966). Flight Safety Foundation (USA).

Routledge, Brigadier (1944). AA command records.

Symposium Report. TSR2 (1998). Royal Air Force Historical Society.

INDEX

Note: Illustrations have *italic* page numbers. There may also be textual references on these pages.